A BHOY'S OWN STORY

A Bhoy's Own Story

Paul Lambert
with
Graham Clark

MAINSTREAM
PUBLISHING

EDINBURGH AND LONDON

First published in Great Britain in 1998 by
MAINSTREAM PUBLISHING COMPANY (EDINBURGH) LTD
7 Albany Street
Edinburgh EH1 3UG

ISBN 1 84018 086 2

A catalogue record for this book is available from the British Library

Typeset in Book Antiqua
Printed and bound in Great Britain by Butler and Tanner Ltd

CONTENTS

ACKNOWLEDGEMENTS

I would like to dedicate this book firstly to those who have been so influential in my family life – my wife Monica, children Christopher and Kira, mum Jeanette, dad Billy and sister Lee, together with my grandparents, Robert and Isa Lambert and David and Rose Sutherland. I also owe a debt of gratitude to my former neighbours in Dortmund – Manny and Doris Neuhaus and Thomas and Birgit Rux. Then, of course, there are those who have helped shape my football career – especially Alex Stephen, Alex Smith, Ottmar Hitzfeld, Michael Henke, Toni Schumacher, Michael Meier and Nevio Scala – and, last but not least, my former team-mates at Borussia Dortmund for making the European dream come true and my present team-mates at Celtic for winning the 1997–98 Premier League championship. Thank you all.

All photographs of me with Celtic and Scotland are courtesy of Steve Welsh. Front cover photo is by Eric McCowat.

1

SAINT AND SINNER

I take nothing for granted in football and I think that stems from my early days at St Mirren when at various times I saw the good, the bad and the ugly side of the game.

Looking back on my time at Love Street, it was an incredible start for a youngster. It was full of highs and lows and more moments of genuine drama than any player has a right to experience throughout his career, never mind in just the first few seasons.

Walk-outs, fires, fights, successes, failures, triumphs and tears punctuated my early days, first as an 'S' form signing for Saints, then as a YTS kid and eventually as a full-time professional. It's a miracle, really, that I'm here to tell the tale! It was, to say the least, a bizarre beginning to my life as a footballer, but I suppose you've got to start somewhere.

Dad Billy and mum Jeanette are responsible for me initially, and although I was born in Glasgow, the family moved to Linwood in Renfrewshire when I was just two.

After that, life was the same for me as it is for millions of youngsters. We played football at every available opportunity, and at different ages I played for Mossedge Primary School, Linwood High School and Linwood Rangers Boys Club.

Obviously I am indebted to my parents first and foremost, but Alex Stephen, who was in charge of the boys club, is another who deserves my thanks. He was a big influence on me and even now he still looks after teams.

I suppose I first thought about football as a career when I, along with my big pal Norrie McWhirter who's now at St Mirren, began to be picked at representative level.

Of all the matches at that time only one really stands out and that was for Scotland at Under-15 level against, naturally, England. I was a striker in those days and I remember John Spencer in that team as well. We lost 4–3 at Nottingham Forest's ground, but it was a great game.

Playing in matches like that inevitably attracts interest, and St Mirren scout Maxie Gray was the first to spot a bit of potential in Norrie and me – although we nearly slipped through the Love Street net.

We were both due to sign for Saints on a Thursday night but clearly no one at the club had been told, so we went home disappointed. But once Maxie heard that nothing had happened he sorted it all out and we put pen to paper the following week.

It was Ricky McFarlane who took us on initially, but we weren't there all that long before Alex Miller took over. It was Alex, indeed, who took me on as a professional and if I hadn't fulfilled that dream then I guess I would have been a roof tiler like my dad. Thank you, Alex!

Saints had a smashing side then. Guys like Campbell Money, Jim Rooney, Frank McAvennie, Ian Scanlon, Billy Abercrombie and Kenny McDowall were all around, and it was great for me, Norrie and Brian Hamilton, who has enjoyed a fine career as well, to be involved with them.

All the while we were also attending college in Motherwell and I suppose it was then that I received my first, but certainly not my last, rollicking from a manager.

The young lads were interested only in football and certainly not in learning about anything else, so when we didn't bother going to college one day we didn't think anyone would be too concerned. How wrong can you be? Alex Miller heard about it and went off his head. He read the riot act and I can now see why.

Alex, together with Martin Ferguson and Drew Jarvie, wanted us to develop the right habits. I guess they had seen plenty of other youngsters go off the rails at that age and they didn't want the same thing to happen to us. They kept us on the straight and narrow.

It can, though, be a frustrating time for kids with ideas above their station. We all felt we were good enough to be knocking on the first-team door practically before we had come through the gates to the stadium, and it took a manager like Miller to make us see sense.

And I can't really complain, because I made my début as a substitute for Saints on 12 April 1986 when I was just 16 – against Motherwell – and we won 2–1.

That was memorable for no one apart from me, but there are thousands upon thousands of people in Paisley and beyond who can look back fondly at the following season.

Alex Smith took over the Love Street hot-seat from Miller, who went to manage Hibs, and I must say he was terrific with the younger players. Indeed, he and assistant Jimmy Bone were a great partnership, with Alex calm and collected and Jimmy demented!

I was in the first-team squad more often than not by then and quite happy to be there because, basically, I felt I should be.

The league season was fairly routine – typical of St Mirren at that time – but the Scottish Cup was something else. The third round – the first for bigger clubs – was fairly straightforward with a 3–0 victory over Inverness Caley.

The next round, though, was a bit more dramatic

because, apart from anything else, it was against Saints' bitter rivals Morton. Celtic against Rangers remains the most talked-about derby match in Scotland – and beyond, for that matter – but Paisley and Greenock enjoy a fair old rivalry as well.

We won that one 3–2 at Cappielow and then travelled to Kirkcaldy, where we beat Raith Rovers 2–0 to move into the semi-finals. It was a big thing, of course, for Saints to get that far even if they had made a bit of a habit of it at the time, but for a youngster like me it was neither here nor there. I was just 17, and at that age you don't know the meaning of pressure. You just want to play and, really, nothing else concerns you. Basically, you haven't a care in the world.

So the semi-final against Hearts didn't faze me one little bit. Nor did Hampden Park. Frank McGarvey scored a cheeky goal to give us a 2–1 victory, and the partying started in earnest – even if I was too young to really get involved!

The season continued relatively uneventfully until the last league match which just happened to be against Rangers at Ibrox – some way to prepare for the following weekend's Cup final against Dundee United.

Rangers had actually won the title by then, and with us doing nothing much in the middle of the table it was all a bit of a carnival, and I was looking forward to it as the last chance to have a run-out before Hampden.

You can imagine, then, how I felt when Alex called me aside before the game and told me he was leaving me out. I was devastated because any player – whoever he is – wants to play all the time.

But in virtually the same breath Alex explained why he wasn't playing me – it was because he was keeping me for the final. I couldn't believe it. The big game was a week away and I was being told I was going to be part of it all. You could say that made up for the disappointment of being left out of the Ibrox match.

In fact, I left a note along with tickets for my dad for the Rangers game and had to explain to him why I wasn't playing at Ibrox. In the circumstances, I don't think he minded too much.

So it was on to the final and I have to say straight off I probably didn't give the occasion the respect it deserved. I was just a kid, and although a lot of the pre-match spotlight fell on younger lads like Brian Hamilton, Ian Ferguson and me, it didn't mean that much to us.

I certainly didn't fully realise its significance and, looking back on it, I think I felt my life would be full of cup finals. I wish. To me, honestly, it was just another game and that's a bit embarrassing in hindsight.

The match itself probably wasn't that great a game either, but when I saw the size of the St Mirren contingent in the crowd I could hardly believe it. I don't know where all those Buddies came from – or, for that matter, where they went afterwards, because they disappeared back into the woodwork as quickly as they had emerged from it!

Still, it was a memorable afternoon for each and every one of them. I was actually taken off and replaced by Tony Fitzpatrick a couple of minutes from the end, and about all I can remember of the actual match is listening to Jimmy Bone having a terrible rant at Ian Ferguson before the start of extra time. He gave him a real doing.

Mind you, it worked, because Fergie went on to score the winner! That sent half of Hampden into raptures, and it was a terrific feeling to have won the Cup.

After it was all over and I went out to meet my dad, I couldn't believe it when I saw he was crying. I was mortified and told him he was giving me a real showing-up, but he turned round and said: 'Do you realise what you've done? If you do, fine. If you don't, you certainly will in the future.'

And that was true because, like I say, I didn't appreciate everything then, but when I think back to grown men in tears, the number of fans who turned out hoping to witness history, and the scenes the following day in Paisley, I know just what was achieved by that team.

Maybe it was all too easy not to appreciate it, though, because when everyone else was busy partying the night away at a Paisley hotel, I was despatched home by the manager because I was too young to drink! It was the biggest day of my footballing life and I was in bed by 10.30 p.m.!

The scenes in the town on the Sunday after the game were incredible. Black and white scarves, banners and hats were everywhere, and it seemed as if the whole of Renfrewshire had turned out to pay tribute to Saints.

That weekend should have been the catalyst for the club to move on to bigger and better things. It should have been a platform for Saints to build upon. It was a great moment that could and should have sparked all sorts of things.

Unfortunately, it wasn't to be. St Mirren didn't even stand still after that historic Cup success – they went backwards, and that is a crime. It was such a waste of a glorious opportunity to move forward.

Still, that is for others to lament. I had a career to get on with, and I had a quiet feeling of satisfaction that I had made a decent start.

After that final I put my medal and a schoolboy cap I had won in a glass case, and I still laugh now when I recall the day I went home to discover that my prized cap had been replaced by an old bunnet. My grandad had a sense of humour even though, sadly, he was very ill around that time.

Indeed, I didn't go on Saints' tour to the Far East that summer because he was so unwell. Instead, I went to see him in Salisbury with a video recording of the Cup final, which he had been too ill to attend. He died not long afterwards, and it remains one of my greatest regrets that he didn't see what I went on to achieve in the game.

There was another tragedy around that time when mum and dad's house was destroyed by a fire. It was terrible and they lost a lot of valuable possessions yet, incredibly, that medal and that cap remained unscathed in the wreckage. It was as close as I have come to a miracle, and it seemed the gods were smiling on me then as they seem to have done through most of my career.

But with St Mirren it was clear I had peaked at an early age and, generally speaking, things went downhill from then on at Love Street.

And it wasn't just for me that things started to go wrong with Saints then. One way and another, a whole host of people were affected. Alex Smith and Jimmy Bone, for instance, didn't last all that much longer despite what they had achieved at the club. And there were others who never hit the same heights again.

Billy Abercrombie was one. He was injured in our first European Cup-Winners' Cup tie against Tromso of Norway and that more or less finished the wee man, who had been a terrific captain.

Europe, of course, was a huge adventure for Saints. Little did I realise, however, what an adventure it would prove to be for me in the future.

We drew Tromso in the first round and Kenny McDowall gave us the perfect start with a goal at Love Street after just three minutes, although we failed to add to that.

I was substituted, being replaced by Paul Chalmers, and I padded off to the dressing-room thinking it was a decent enough start, even if it had all been a bit low-key.

I was sitting on my own going over the game as players do when, all of a sudden, Frank McGarvey joined me, cursing the fact that he had been taken off. Frank was raging because he felt he had had a good game and it was clear he wasn't best pleased to have made way for Norrie McWhirter late on.

Still, even his outburst didn't prepare me for what happened next. The door burst open yet again and in stormed assistant boss Jimmy Bone, who delivered a sharp warning to Frank never to question his decisions again – and then hooked him! Honestly, Mike Tyson would have been proud of the punch. It was a belter.

Remember, I was a naïve young lad and I have to admit I couldn't quite believe what was happening in front of me as Jimmy and Frank tore into each other. It was an incredible scene as they battled with each other around the dressing-room. I didn't know what to do. Eventually I went out and mentioned that World War III had erupted inside, and various bodies went in to separate the pair.

It was an astonishing scene. It was also my first dressing-room bust-up and undoubtedly one of the reasons behind the departure of Jimmy and Alex Smith not too long afterwards.

Before they went, though, we managed to get through the tie against Tromso intact. We then met Mechelen from Belgium, who proved to be a terrific team and introduced me to yet more about life in Europe.

We had to travel for the first game, and I was particularly impressed when we arrived at their ground to see a long line of Peugeots belonging to their players. I also remember seeing their players inside dressed in jeans and having a quiet cigarette before the big match!

During the match I recall Irwin Koeman spitting on me, which I didn't much appreciate then and wouldn't now if anyone did it. It's a disgusting habit that certainly has no place in football.

Somehow we got through the night with a 0–0 draw, although quite how we did it remains a mystery to this day. They had terrific players like Preud'homme, Koeman, de Boer and Ohana, and they gave us a real doing.

It was Ohana, in fact, who scored twice in the return at Love Street to leave us down and out, although it was some consolation when the much-underrated Mechelen went on to beat Ajax 1–0 – Danny Blind, Dennis Bergkamp and all – in the final to lift the Cup-Winners' Cup.

On a personal level things weren't going much better, as

Tony Fitzpatrick and Frank McGarvey took over from Alex and Jimmy. It broke my heart when Alex Smith called the lads out on to the park and told us he was going. Others were equally upset, and probably only Tony and Frank weren't. It all went a bit pear-shaped for me then and I was bombed out of the side near the end of the season.

I know around that time that Alex Smith, by now in charge at Aberdeen, wanted to take me to Pittodrie but he felt, not unreasonably, that Saints' asking price of £750,000 for an 18-year-old was a bit steep.

I heard about that unofficially as no one at Love Street had the decency to inform me about the Dons' interest. On top of being dropped, it was about the last straw for me. I decided then that I had had enough. I walked out on Saints and prepared for a life outside football. I was ready to join my dad. I was completely fed up and had lost all respect for Fitzpatrick. It was a difficult time.

I don't know if I would have been a loss to football, but I would certainly have been lost without it. Two things made me change my mind after about a week. The first was that I had no great desire to spend the rest of my life as a roof tiler, and the second was that there was no way I was going to let Fitzpatrick beat me. I hated Tony with a passion at that time, but in hindsight I learned a lesson from the whole saga and it made me more determined than ever to succeed in football.

Things did pick up a bit after that, and at the start of season 1990–91 I was fortunate to be picked for the Scottish League team for the League's centenary match against Scotland at Hampden. It was an interesting side and included players like Pat Bonner, Theo Snelders, Freddy van der Hoorn, Miodrag Krivokapic, Gary Stevens and Chris Morris! Still, we won 1–0 courtesy of a Hans Gillhaus penalty.

We received a medal and £400 for appearing in that centenary match, and it was a nice way for me to start a season that turned out to be a remarkable one for Saints, even if it wasn't very successful. Fitzpatrick stunned Scottish football by signing two players I must admit I never expected for a moment to see at Love Street. Steve Archibald and Victor arrived in Paisley to the astonishment of just about everyone but I have to say, from my point of view, that both were terrific. They were vastly experienced professionals and they went out of their way to help me whenever possible – although, as I discovered to my cost, they weren't above a little bending of the laws.

The two of them – both millionaires, I suspect – decided to challenge Norrie McWhirter and me to a game of tennis with Geordie Shaw as the umpire. Now, the Spaniard was clearly a bit of a shark at the game and was well able to look after himself on a court, whereas Stevie wasn't quite so talented. Norrie and I, well, we could just about get by.

So the scene was set and the stakes – or should that be steaks – were high with a meal at no less a place than the Grosvenor Hotel in Glasgow the prize for the winners, with the losers paying.

Steve's worst failing of all was his service and when it came to the crunch and they were just a game away from beating us he should have been serving for the match. But he and Victor switched roles and the Spaniard served successfully to win. It was only afterwards that we realised we had been conned and Geordie, needless to say, hadn't noticed either.

Honestly, it was a disgrace. They had money coming out of their ears yet we, two struggling pros, had to buy them their dinner. They must be embarrassed about that even now.

Victor, though, was a great guy, even though he once failed to see the funny side of it when Geordie cut the toes off his socks in the dressing-room!

Neither of them, however, could save us from an abysmal season. Tony eventually resigned, to be replaced by David Hay who, to be honest, didn't fare much better. The follow-ing season was equally disastrous and we couldn't score goals to save our lives. I think at one point we went eight games without a goal, which tells you where our problems lay. Relegation wasn't pleasant, but it was hardly a shock.

Maybe unsurprisingly, that prompted another managerial change, with Jimmy Bone taking over the very hot Love Street seat.

I must admit that the prospect of the First Division didn't appeal to me. There's no atmosphere at games, the grounds aren't as good and the standard isn't that clever, and when you put all those things together it wasn't a very attractive proposition.

So that's why I jumped at the chance to talk to Dundee United after Jimmy had agreed a deal with Jim McLean. When I got to Tannadice, however, it didn't feel quite right – and that was nothing to do with the fact that I couldn't even get past the security gate!

But when I did I felt I had to listen to what Mr McLean had to say, and I did that. To be fair, he sold the club well. The money was good and he offered me a three-year deal that included a big signing-on fee. I had the medical that Thursday and I genuinely felt I would sign, despite a few misgivings.

Jim wanted an early decision because they were starting the season against Motherwell and he wanted me in the team. So the pressure was on as I headed back home and, to be frank, I must have changed my mind a thousand times. That night I couldn't sleep for trying to decide what to do and the next morning – the Friday – my dad came down and told me simply to go with my gut feeling.

Even then I struggled to come to a decision, and I went into Love Street for a chat with Jimmy Bone and told him I still didn't have a clue what to do. Jimmy was very good about it and simply told me to go out and get a breath of fresh air and think about it some more. He said he would be happy for me whatever the outcome was. I had to admit that my initial doubts had always been there, and finally I decided that United wasn't the right club for me.

Jimmy duly phoned Jim McLean to tell him, and I got on with my life after a tortuous 48 hours. Maybe United had the last laugh, though, because we started our First Division campaign by being beaten 7–0 by Raith Rovers at Stark's Park and were then knocked out of the Skol Cup – at Tannadice – a couple of weeks later!

Happily we improved, although we still missed out on promotion behind Raith Rovers, Kilmarnock and Dunfermline, and it wasn't all plain sailing for me.

I recall one major bust-up with Jimmy Bone and, looking back at it now, I was bang out of order even if, at the time, I was in no doubt at all that I was right to take the stand I did. I was captain of Saints then and maybe I had a higher opinion of myself than I should have done.

Whatever the reason, when I was picked to play in a Friday friendly against a team from Iceland, I declared that there was no way I wanted to play in the league match against Stirling Albion the following day. Basically, I was in a huff.

Jimmy and I had a huge blow-out over it, and I remember him labelling me a 'big-time Charlie' among other things! In fact, we didn't speak for a couple of weeks afterwards and it all became a bit nasty.

Eventually, however, I calmed down and saw the error of my ways. I realised I had been totally unprofessional and, apart from anything else, I knew there was only one winner in a situation like that and that was the manager. So I apologised and returned to the side immediately. It was just another part of the learning process, even if it was a bit of a sore lesson for me.

The following year began just as the previous one had – with an offer from Dundee United to go to Tannadice. This time it was from Ivan Golac, who had taken over from Jim McLean, and I ended up going to Tayside for a week, playing a friendly match for them and being told that they would keep an eye on me!

If they had made me another offer I'm not sure I would

have rejected it again because I don't think I could have handled another season in the First Division. As it happened, though, I didn't have to because I was nearing my final days as a Saint – and, admittedly, sometimes a sinner – anyway.

2

MOTHERWELL AND ME

I was so fed up playing in the First Division I would have signed for just about anyone at the start of season 1993–94, so when I received a phone call from Jimmy Bone telling me that Tommy McLean wanted to see me at Motherwell I wasted no time in heading for Lanarkshire.

I had started the term at Love Street but I have to admit the prospect of another full season – with no guarantee of promotion for Saints – filled me with a sense of despair.

I know that's probably wrong but I was 24 by then. I was ambitious and I had done my time in Paisley. In fact, there were times when I felt I had maybe spent too long at Love Street. I was in a rut. I knew it, and so too, probably, did Jimmy Bone. The time was right for me to move on.

So the invitation from another McLean was just what I wanted to hear, although he obviously didn't sign me because of my form immediately prior to that time. I discovered, for instance, that Willie McLean – the third of the famous brothers who was also on the Motherwell staff

– had watched me in a match a bit earlier when I had lasted just three minutes before being sent off for elbowing Morton's Jim Tolmie!

They must have taken previous form – if you'll pardon the expression – into account and I'm eternally grateful for that. And – I think I'm safe telling Tommy McLean this now – I would have put pen to paper on virtually whatever deal he had put in front of me. I didn't mention that at the time, mind you!

It at least meant there was no real problem over the terms Tommy offered me, but even so there was a potential snag with the transfer because Jim Gardner was part of the deal. He was to go to Love Street while I headed in the opposite direction and my problem was that I didn't know whether or not Jim was as desperate to complete his part as I was mine.

While I was busy trying to get my name down on the contract as quickly as possible and before anyone changed their mind, Jim was in the room next door discussing terms with Jimmy Bone and Saints director Bob Earlie. I had already been told the whole thing was off if Jim didn't agree and I have to say it was a bit of a sweat knowing my future was in someone else's hands.

Fortunately, the whole affair fell into place and Tommy outlined his plans to me. He also knew I was going nowhere at Love Street so he emphasised the point that he was offering me a new platform and that it was up to me thereafter.

That was fine by me because, when all the i's were dotted and the t's crossed, I took stock and realised, apart from anything else, that my value had plummeted in the previous 12 months or so. At one stage previously, Tony Fitzpatrick had put a price of something like £750,000 on my head. Then Tommy's brother Jim had been looking to pay around £350,000, and now I was heading to Fir Park for about £100,000 plus Jim Gardner. It was a sobering reminder of how bad things had become.

Looking back on that long spell at Love Street, I often wonder if success came too early for me with that Scottish Cup victory. I think after that I expected Saints to go from strength to strength and when it didn't happen there was a real feeling of anti-climax. And the longer we went without achieving anything, the worse it all became. I had such great expectations after 1987. Having said that, I appreciated what I had learned through all my trials and tribulations at the Paisley club and it certainly prepared me well for the rest of my career.

Motherwell, though, represented a new and exciting challenge and at last I was ready to kick-start my football life once more.

I started off with a reserve game when Tom Forsyth and Davie Cooper looked after the lads and then I made my début against Hearts when, happily, we won 2–0 with goals from Phil O'Donnell and Paul McGrillen. I even hit the bar. It was a satisfactory start.

Unfortunately, it didn't continue in the same vein and we immediately went on a run of three games when we couldn't score for love nor money. In the middle of that spell wee Tam brought in a psychologist to speak to the players, but I have to confess I wasn't particularly impressed with what he said. Mind you, maybe he did the trick because after those three barren matches we went to Ibrox and won 2–1 after Dougie Arnott came off the bench and scored both goals! Maybe our failure *was* in the mind . . .

There's no doubt that that result against Rangers lifted everyone's confidence. We had a good team anyway, but after that the lads started to believe in themselves and each other, and our season took off big-style.

The team hardly changed, which was a bonus. The only way you can get consistency with results is with consistency of selection, and, basically, Tommy McLean put out the same 11 every week. The team generally was: Sieb Dykstra, Rab Shannon, Rab McKinnon, Miodrag Krivokapic, Brian Martin, Chris McCart, yours truly, Jamie Dolan, Dougie

Arnott, Phil O'Donnell and Tommy Coyne. Others in and around the squad were Stevie Kirk, Paul McGrillen and John Philliben.

It was a pleasure playing in that team – particularly after struggling with Saints. We really did play some outstanding football and pushed Rangers all the way for the Premier League championship, which was no mean achievement for 'Well.

It wasn't all sweetness and light, though. How could it be, when one of the McLeans was in charge? Tommy was a terrific manager but he certainly wasn't above the occasional tantrum if things didn't go his way. Stories about him – and, for that matter, Jim – are legendary, and I found out why after a game against Partick Thistle.

We were leading 2–1 with just a couple of minutes left when I thought we had the chance to add a third. I picked the ball up and tried to play Dougie Arnott in at the edge of their area, but instead I succeeded only in giving the ball away to Chic Charnley. He promptly moved it on to Roddy Grant, who scored the equaliser. It's at times like that you would happily disappear into a big hole if one appeared.

Instead, though, the final whistle went and I headed for the tunnel. I was expecting the worst anyway, but my case certainly wasn't helped by Chic, who followed me and shouted just loud enough for wee Tam to hear: 'Thanks for that goal, Paul.' It was just what I needed!

When I reached the dressing-room I waited for the explosion but instead suffered what was probably worse – near silence. Tommy walked about and eventually, instead of shouting and bawling as I had expected, launched into a really sarcastic outburst that left me feeling about a foot tall. Come to think of it, his last sentence was: 'You can't be a wee boy out there forever.' Honestly, I think I would have preferred a volley of abuse.

Still, Tommy and 'Well had proved a good mix, and when I look back at that season now I feel we were actually a bit unlucky not to win the league.

That's why it was a huge shock to us all when we heard that McLean had resigned. I'm not sure what went wrong for him at Fir Park but the feeling then, and it was probably accurate, was that he wasn't given sufficient money to spend. That is always going to be a problem at Motherwell.

In that instance, though, it was a real shame because if Tommy had been able to add a couple of players to his squad, who knows what might have been achieved? As it was, things went from good to better but not quite to best.

I was in the Fir Park dressing-room when I heard about the successor to Tommy and there's no point in denying I was very, very surprised to learn it was Alex McLeish who was coming as player-manager.

I had played against Eck, of course, but I couldn't have said I knew him when he took over. What I did know, however, was that Tommy McLean would be a hard act to follow.

Alex started well enough and, to be fair to him, there was a bit more humour about Fir Park with him as boss than there had been with McLean. He also took a quick look around and clearly decided that the squad that had done so well the previous year didn't need tampering with that much. It was his first shrewd decision and it paid dividends.

First things first, though, and that, strangely, meant a European tie before a ball had been kicked in earnest in domestic football. That really was a bit unreal, although it has to be said that it's taken me until now to master the name of the opposition we faced then. It was Havnar Boltfealg from the Faroe Islands.

Unusual name. Unusual tie. We were still struggling for match fitness when we played the first game at Fir Park but we won comfortably enough, and if the second leg wasn't quite a formality then we still went to the Faroes with plenty of confidence.

Maybe that was just as well, because the Faroes provided me with something a bit different . . . like grass roofs. Or like travelling to the game by bus and boat. Or like being so cold that even brass monkeys would have been concerned. And, remember, this was in August!

All that was bad enough, but I didn't actually play in the return game and had to sit on the bench, freezing, as the rest of the lads did the business. Then, to compound everything, I was chosen to take the drugs test. I managed, but I remember thinking at the time that I was lucky everything was still intact by then, it was so cold!

If that preliminary-round tie was memorable for a variety of reasons, the first round proper was totally unforgettable because, although I didn't know it at the time, the draw that paired Motherwell with mighty Borussia Dortmund was to turn my career upside down.

Much more of that later, but it was, anyway, a terrific tie for us. I remember Michael Henke, Dortmund's co-trainer, coming over to watch us in a game at Rugby Park. He actually went down to Kilmarnock with us on the team bus but he must have been killing himself laughing after he saw us. We won 1–0 but we were dreadful, and when he headed back to Germany he couldn't possibly have been too concerned about the prospects.

And it's equally hard to imagine what he thought about me personally because I was struggling. Monica, my wife, was expecting our first child at the time and I was quite concerned about that, so much so that it was affecting my form. So much so, indeed, that I told Alex McLeish there was no way I was going to Germany for the UEFA Cup tie if Monica hadn't given birth by then. I don't think he was best pleased when I mentioned that fact but, while football is obviously very important to me, it is not, as Bill Shankly once said, more important than life or death. My family came first then, as it does now.

Christopher, as the baby was to be named, was actually due on the same day as the Borussia game and there was no way I was going to miss the birth. I wanted to be there. Maybe that was the start of things going a bit wrong between me and Alex. I don't think our relationship ever truly recovered.

Having said that my family came first, we had a game even before the trip, against Dundee United at Tannadice, and Monica had the baby at three o'clock on the Saturday morning, which was great – even if he was a bit late. I left the hospital at five and had a bit of breakfast at home before returning to see Monica and the new addition. Billy Davies came to pick me up, and even though I had had no sleep I played in the 1–1 draw against United.

So it was a tired but happy Paul Lambert who travelled to Germany with the rest of the lads, and when we trained at the Westfalen Stadium I must admit I felt like a new player. The surroundings helped, of course, because the ground was spectacular.

The whole occasion was brilliant and room-mate Rab McKinnon and I couldn't believe our eyes on the morning of the game when we saw Dortmund city centre come alive with fans. You can imagine, then, what the place was like nearer kick-off, and I savoured every minute of it all because I assumed it would be the only time in my life I would be in the Westfalen Stadium. How wrong can you be?

Still, it was a memorable night for a variety of reasons, among them the few minutes we were in the tunnel waiting to go out. We had done a good warm-up and I was sweating a lot. I looked across at the Dortmund lads and in particular at Julio Cesar, who was playing his first game back after injury. Honestly, I couldn't believe what I was seeing – or smelling! What I was looking at was a giant of a guy carefully fixing his hair, and what I was smelling was an overdose of aftershave! I'll never forget that moment.

I'll never forget, either, the fact that we made a real game of it. We had a few good chances. Tommy Coyne, Rab and myself all missed opportunities and I felt we were really unlucky to lose 1–0 to an Andy Möller goal not long after half-time. We had Paul McGrillen sent off but we certainly gave them a fright, that's for sure. I was up against Michael Zorc and enjoyed our battle. Later – much later – I used to laugh with him about how I had him in my pocket that night.

It was, however, an important night for both myself and Motherwell because we gained an enormous amount of self-belief from our performance against a side as good as Dortmund. They proved exactly how good in the return at Fir Park, where Karl-Heinz Riedle scored twice to leave us dead and buried. On top of that, we had Rab Shannon and Dougie Arnott sent off to complete a miserable picture.

There were lighter moments too, like when Andy Möller came into our dressing-room afterwards and not only changed jerseys with Jamie Dolan but gave our midfield man his entire kit. We took the mick out of Jamie when we asked if he got Andy's knickers as well!

But the two games were a terrific experience generally and we learned a lot from them. In fact, we drew our next match against Celtic and then proceeded to win five on the trot, including victories over Rangers, Aberdeen and Hearts.

It was a magnificent season, all in all. For a club the size of Motherwell it was a remarkable effort to go one better than the previous year and finish second. Alex didn't change much at all. He brought in Stevie Woods and sold Phil O'Donnell, but otherwise he stuck with Tommy McLean's team.

The same couldn't be said the following season when McLeish decided to make changes – and maybe even for the sake of change. It was difficult to see any other reason. The Fir Park manager eventually sold Rab Shannon and then swapped Stevie Kirk and Paul McGrillen for Falkirk's Eddie May, which I think it's fair to say surprised a lot of people. Both Stevie and Paul had done the club a real turn over the years.

That pre-season we went to Holland, and as bad preparations go it was pretty grim from the very beginning.

We were on the wrong end of a real doing from NEC, when their players were flying past us for fun. Rab Shannon and I were on the same side of the park that day, and I remember us looking at each other and wondering what was going on. I'll never know how we escaped from that one with a 1–1 draw.

Obviously the management weren't best pleased with the performance, and when Tommy Coyne and I were standing outside the dressing-room we could hear Alex and assistant Andy Watson giving Jamie Dolan some terrible stick.

Next time it was my turn after I had been booked, admittedly stupidly, for throwing the ball away during a match against a Belgian team. When Alex walked up to me afterwards, I thought he was going to hook me. He was livid. He started calling me for everything and we had a huge row.

Billy Davies was next in the firing line, at half-time during the game against Wolfsburg, and I think a few of us realised then that things were going downhill rapidly. It just seemed to some of us that the manager was picking on players the previous boss had signed.

The situation was far from ideal and it was clear pretty early on that season that we might struggle. In fact, at one point we went something like eight games without even scoring a goal. Things were not good.

I had yet another bust-up with McLeish that season at the training ground. Once more, I hold my hands up now and say it was a bit unprofessional of me, but it was as much to do with frustration as anything. At least I played in virtually every game, though, so I can't say I was left out of the picture, despite the various run-ins I had.

Not that the season ever looked like being as good as the previous ones, and eventually the fact that we stayed up at all was virtually down to the signing of Willie Falconer. He arrived around the start of the new year and scored some vital goals to help the cause.

Apart from trying to avoid relegation, there was another pressing matter attracting my attention – my contract was up in the summer and around March I started talking to the club about the possibilities. To be more accurate, Jim Melrose, my agent at the time, began negotiations. Unfortunately – or maybe fortunately, as it turned out – it wasn't long before it became fairly obvious that Jim and I weren't on the same wavelength as the club. Once that had been discovered, and with the new Bosman ruling in place that made me a free agent when my current deal expired, I told Jim to go out and get me a club.

Rab McKinnon was in the same position and after a deal fell through that would have taken him to Aberdeen, he eventually took advantage of the Bosman ruling and signed for Twente Enschede in Holland.

McLeish, meanwhile, phoned me to say he could get me more money, but it was a paltry sum and I knew that Motherwell's valuation of me didn't match my own. Not even nearly.

The writing was on the wall, and when I saw what McKinnon had done with his life, not only did I begin to feel more and more that my future lay away from Fir Park, the prospect of going continental also became more and more appealing.

There are lots of things that happen behind the scenes in any transfer deal. Some good, some bad, some indifferent. When it comes to players moving on, you tend to find out exactly what your manager thinks of you – and it's not always complimentary. When I informed Alex McLeish that I hoped to continue my career abroad, he didn't actually laugh in my face but he made it clear he thought it unlikely, to say the least. He told me: 'You're a home bird – you'll never do that.'

What Alex didn't know, though, was that by then I had already spoken to an agent on the continent and he had asked me to give him a couple of weeks to have a look around and see what was happening. He came back to me fairly quickly and let me know there were a couple of clubs showing interest.

It was what I wanted to hear, even if it struck me that they were unlikely to be big names in a European context. The best I was really hoping for was teams from the lower reaches of the Dutch or Belgian first divisions.

That's why I was absolutely flabbergasted when I was informed that the two clubs were, wait for it, PSV Eindhoven and Borussia Dortmund – two seriously big clubs from Holland and Germany. I was amazed – and delighted. It opened up a whole new world of dreams and I knew there and then that I couldn't pass up the opportunity.

I told myself over and over again that this was going to be a case of nothing ventured, nothing gained. I had to give it my best shot, because opportunities like the one I was being presented with, I realised only too well, didn't come along too often.

So, basically, I went sick. Monica phoned Fir Park to tell them I wasn't feeling well. When McLeish returned from training he phoned the house and was actually a bit stroppy with Monica. I think he may have suspected something was up. But by then I didn't care, and I told him I wasn't well enough to go south on a pre-season trip, which, as you might imagine, went down like the *Titanic*.

I was preparing to pack my bags, certainly, but my destination was altogether different from that of the rest of the Motherwell lads. I was off to Holland. Eindhoven, to be precise.

3

TRIALS . . . AND TRIBULATIONS

Dick Advocaat is now firmly installed as boss of Rangers and is plotting the downfall of the club I play for. It's astonishing how things work out because there was a time not so very long ago when the Dutchman might have signed me. Indeed, I believe that, as things turned out, he might even now have a slight regret he didn't.

But that's jumping the gun. It came to pass that summer that I was on the smallest plane ever designed and manu- factured, going from Amsterdam to Enschede on a quiet summer's day. Honestly, the aircraft was the size of my dining-room table, and the fact that there was just one other passenger on board maybe tells you that the locals knew what that particular flight was like.

Still, I could have flown there myself, I was on such a high at the prospect of what lay ahead. I was on cloud nine anyway, even though my future was far from clear-cut.

There were certainly no guarantees in front of me but I knew that, whatever the outcome of the following few days, I would have to give it my best shot.

I was set to go to PSV and, depending on how things worked out in Holland, on to Dortmund. It was a mouth-watering thought even if, at the same time, I was scared stiff I might blow it.

I knew from conversations with Billy Davies at Fir Park that Alex McLeish had made it clear to the rest of the Motherwell lads that he thought I was wasting my time, and although that irritated me a bit I didn't give it too much thought. I had enough on my plate worrying about that short hop to Enschede.

My agent, Ton van Dalen, picked me up at the small airport and we drove to the training camp PSV were at. The Eindhoven coach was, of course, Advocaat, who met us at the hotel, and he quickly outlined to me what he was looking for.

It was probably a lost cause even then, because Dick wanted a player to play wide on the right, get to the byline and knock over crosses which, to be fair, wasn't exactly my game. But I didn't say too much because the opportunity was still there and I wasn't about to blow it without even attempting to do the job. I knew I was no Jimmy Johnstone, mind you.

It's a slightly strange situation to go on trial to a big club like that anyway, because it's only something that has started regularly since the Bosman ruling. The rest of the Eindhoven players were in their beds when I arrived because they had a game that night, but I must say when I met them they were all terrific.

They spoke English, which helped, but generally they were very welcoming to a complete stranger, and all the big names were there – Luc Nilis, Marc Degryse, Wim Jonk, Arthur Numan, Philip Cocu and Jaap Stam.

I played in the match against a local amateur team on the biggest park in the world and on the warmest night of that summer, and we won 12–1. I scored and felt I did quite well although really it was no occasion to judge anyone. Afterwards I remember Numan – now, of course, at Rangers – being particularly friendly, and he too seemed to think I had done okay.

The following day, though, was murder, even if it did give me an insight into how Mr Advocaat works. For a start, we had to cycle to training, which was an interesting beginning to the day. After that we did an enormous amount of running. We went around a forest and we ran on a kind of motocross track full of sand. It was seriously hard work. Yet there wasn't a murmur of discontent, and everyone went about their business with a professionalism that I must admit I hadn't witnessed before. It was a bit of a shock to the system one way and another.

Then we played another match and I scored again in a 3–2 victory, although I have to add I wasn't under any illusions about what I had done in the game.

After that we went back to the hotel and Advocaat, who knew I was going on from there to Dortmund, asked me to go up to see him. When I did, he was very good, very honest and very straight about the whole thing. He told me that if he had been looking for a central midfielder he would have taken me, but that he needed someone for a different role. He then wished me luck and that was it.

I have absolutely no complaint with him about anything and, indeed, when I bumped into him again some time later when I was a regular in the Borussia team he simply shook his head ruefully and indicated that maybe he should have taken me on after all.

It was, though, disappointing, and although I was happy to be heading for another attempt at Dortmund, I vowed there and then that that would be my last try at getting myself a club abroad. It's hard for a player to prove himself in these circumstances and it really isn't ideal, so I told myself: no more trials after Borussia. If I suffered another knock-back, that was that.

I knew that the alternative was returning to Motherwell with my tail firmly between my legs – a prospect McLeish might have relished to the full – but it was something I had to think about. If I had to return, I would sign monthly deals and hope for something else to come up.

So it was with those thoughts in mind that I headed for Germany to be met at the Westfalen Stadium by general manager Michael Meier. At least I had a bit of history with Borussia, having played against them in the UEFA Cup, but that was never going to be enough and I knew that.

Mr Meier, however, told me that the club needed a midfield player because of bad injuries to Steffen Freund and Paulo Sousa, and when he mentioned names like these I realised all of a sudden just what I was trying to get myself into. Freund had just been part of Germany's victorious European Championship side in England and Sousa was, of course, an established Portuguese international.

Yet they were just the tip of the iceberg at Borussia. The players at the club read like a Who's Who of top stars. Here was this wee guy from Linwood trying to grab a place in amongst the likes of those two, Michael Zorc, Matthias Sammer, Karl-Heinz Riedle, Lars Ricken, Stefan Reuter, Andy Möller, Jurgen Kohler, Stefan Klos, Julio Cesar, Heiko Herrlich, Jorg Heinrich and Stephane Chapuisat. It was bizarre.

When Michael Meier reeled off some of the names in the squad, I must admit I felt a bit out of my depth. Still, he put in front of me a deal that would become a firm contract if coach Ottmar Hitzfeld wanted me after my trial period, and I have to confess it was beyond my wildest dreams. I don't suppose it was very much compared to some of the afore-mentioned big guns but, believe me, it compared more than favourably with my Motherwell wages of £420 a week plus £500 a game if we were in the top four in the Premier League.

The basic wage was by those standards massive, but it was the bonuses that made me catch my breath. They were astronomical, depending on the success of the club.

Having said that, and it might take some believing, I wasn't that interested in the money side of things. Of course it's important but at that stage I was just trying to take in what a chance I had. Borussia had told me I was there for five days, during which time I couldn't sign for anyone else, and that it was up to me.

Five days. Less than a week to settle my future. It was quite daunting but I was more and more determined with every passing minute that I was going to be up for it.

I was, though, more than a bit nervous about the whole thing and those nerves frayed even more when I was taken to join the rest of the Borussia squad in Lubeck, which was four hours from Dortmund.

A guy called Walter Mass drove me there. Now, Walter is about 60 years old, around five foot tall and a real character. We were in Lubeck in about two and a half hours, having travelled the autobahns at speeds upwards of 150 miles per hour. You can maybe imagine the state I was in when we arrived. I was in Lubeck but I was also all over the place!

We went to the local airport, where the squad were arriving from a training camp in Switzerland, and, as I had been once before when Motherwell had played Dortmund, I was astonished to see so many fans around.

Ottmar Hitzfeld introduced himself and told me to get on the team bus, where I met a Romanian lad who was there trying to earn himself a future as well. He was a central defender with Steaua Bucharest but I was so concerned about myself that I can't even remember his name.

We were introduced to the rest of the lads and when we reached the hotel, Michael Zorc – my opponent in the Motherwell tie – made a point of wishing me well, which I appreciated.

My first action for Borussia was 45 minutes against Lubeck followed by another 45 minutes against Hamburg in an interesting three-way session. I simply tried to do my best but it was all a bit unreal because a lot of the players were either injured or enjoying a few extra days' holiday after Euro '96 and didn't play.

We then flew to Dortmund, where Hitzfeld drove the Romanian and me to the Hotel Lennhof, and the coach seemed to be quite happy with my efforts. He also told the pair of us that we would be picked up the next morning for training.

When the driver turned up the next day his passenger was wearing a baseball cap and sunglasses and had an earpiece in. He turned round, shook hands with the Romanian and me and introduced himself as Paulo Sousa! He then spent the entire journey on the car phone. That was my introduction to one of the greatest players in the world!

When I saw the training ground I knew beyond any shadow of a doubt that this was where I wanted to play my football. It was spectacular. The players all had their own lockers and their training kit was laid out meticulously. Fir Park it wasn't.

We had couple of days' training but then I had to say to Michael Meier that I needed to go home to get some clothes and money and, indeed, see the family, which was no problem to them. He then said that I should bring my wife Monica and son Christopher back with me when I returned which, I must admit, gave me a real boost. I felt then, for the first time, that maybe I had a chance.

In my brief trip home I spoke to Alex McLeish but I wish I hadn't bothered. I told him I would be taking the opportunity if it came along, but I must admit he planted a few seeds of doubt in my mind. I don't really know even now what his problem was, but it was clear he didn't think I would make it.

Anyway, we went back out to Germany for what amounted to a make-or-break few days for me. My next outing was to be against Schalke in the Fuji Cup competition that also included Borussia Moenchengladbach and

Bayern Munich and I discovered then that German players, like footballers the world over, are superstitious. On the coach on the way to the game I sat down and was quickly told I couldn't sit in that particular seat because all the players had their own individual places on match days. I had chosen the one Stefan Klos always had, so I moved over to the seat that became my own from then on.

What I then thought would be pre-season games turned out to be something else entirely. It was a bit like Celtic v. Rangers. The stadium was packed with fans and the players all stressed to me how important the game against Schalke was. They had just bought Johan de Kock and Jiri Nemec while we were still a bit under strength, and we lost 3–1. Möller scored a sensational goal for us and I realised then just how special he is.

The dressing-room afterwards was like a morgue. Scottish players are never that concerned when they lose pre-season matches, but this was obviously a major blow to Borussia.

The next game was the third- and fourth-place play-off against Moenchengladbach. We had Kohler back for the first time since Euro '96 and it was, basically, my last chance. I was looking for a good performance, but what I got instead was an ankle injury after 20 minutes. I couldn't believe it. Hitzfeld immediately took me off and I felt as if the world had crashed around me. It was a desperate moment.

We returned to the hotel and on the way all sorts of thoughts were going through my head. I had visions of having to face Alex McLeish knowing I had failed, and that wasn't a pleasant thought. I also felt it had been the chance of a lifetime and it had slipped through my fingers. It was a pretty rotten time, one way and another.

That was a Thursday, and the following day I trained as usual with no hint about my future. Then, out of the blue, Michael Henke, who was Borussia's co-trainer, called me over and said I had to go for a medical because my contract was drawn up and waiting for me to sign it. It was as simple and straightforward as that.

Well, I say 'simple' but the medical was actually a bit serious. When I signed for Motherwell from St Mirren, it had been fairly simple. In Dortmund, on the other hand, they did blood tests, X-rays, scans and even measured my legs. And when it was all over they didn't even tell me the result.

So I had another sleepless night. On the Saturday morning, however, Ottmar Hitzfeld spoke to me, said that everything was in place and told me that no matter what happened in Dortmund it would be invaluable experience for me.

That was enough. The contract was signed and I was delighted. No, more than that, I was ecstatic. I was joining one of the biggest clubs in the world and although there were certainly no guarantees I had at least come that far.

The deal was, as I've said, remarkable and included a house that Patrik Berger had been living in prior to his move to Liverpool, as well as flights home for me and the family. It was like Christmas Day, a birthday and a lottery success rolled into one, and it took a bit of getting used to. But once I had managed to get my head round the idea, I vowed that I would take Hitzfeld's words to heart. I knew it was the chance of a lifetime and I meant to make it count. I told Monica that I was going to learn from the great players around me, even if it was only in training rather than in matches.

I knew I was there to make up the numbers because Borussia had one or two injuries, and I realised only too well that none of the squad saw me as a serious threat to their places. That was fine, because I didn't harbour any delusions of grandeur about myself or about the possibilities that might arise. On paper they were endless, but in real terms I signed a three-year contract knowing that my chances of playing regular first-team football were limited, to say the least. All the while, though, I knew too that it was a gamble I had to take if I was to improve and learn.

So when I joined the squad for the first time as a team-mate, it was a big day for me. The lads all knew I had signed and wished me well, and I roomed with the Russian Vladimir But before my first game, which was a German Cup tie against SG Wattenscheid.

It wasn't the memorable début I would have liked, because I didn't get on until the second half of extra-time and we ended up being beaten 4–3 in what was a significant shock in German football. We still weren't at full strength by any means, but it was nevertheless a very poor result for a team of Borussia's standing, and the dressing-room afterwards reflected that. It was very quiet.

After that I had the chance to return to Scotland and I did see Alex McLeish briefly to tell him it was an opportunity I simply had to take. I don't think he was too happy because, apart from anything else, the Bosman ruling meant Motherwell received no money for me.

When I went back out I prepared myself for my new life. Monica had to do all the hard work in terms of shipping out our furniture and the like, and gradually I settled into a whole new world.

I did a few media interviews at the training ground but I was a very small fish in a big pond, and when you can speak to players who had won the Bundesliga two seasons on the trot – including half of Germany's European Cham-pionship team – you're not likely to want too many words of wisdom from a Scot from Motherwell.

Still, I had arrived, and I was number 14 in a first-team squad of 25. I was back on that cloud nine again.

4

THE ROAD TO MUNICH

When I first arrived at Borussia Dortmund I looked around the players in the squad and, believe it or not, actually had a premonition we would win the European Cup.

Call me Mystic Meg or whatever you like, but I knew within days of signing for the German champions that the season that lay ahead would probably offer me the chance of a lifetime to win the biggest club honour in the game.

I only had to look around at my team-mates to believe we could do it. They were all there – Jurgen Kohler, Stephane Chapuisat, Stefan Reuter, Andy Möller, Matthias Sammer, Paulo Sousa, Jorg Heinrich, Steffen Freund, Michael Zorc, Julio Cesar, Stefan Klos, and so on. The squad, I reasoned, had to be at least as good as, if not better than, any other in the tournament.

In the end I was, of course, proved right, but it was a long and winding road to the final in Munich and it was eventful, to say the least. On that incredible roller-coaster ride I came up against players of the quality of Milinko

Pantic, Diego Simeone, Sabri Lamouchi, Moussa Saib, Ryan Giggs and Eric Cantona, I helped dump Manchester United and silence their arrogant media hype and I made more money than I had ever dreamt of. Oh, I also nearly got arrested – and all that before we even reached the final!

The whole incredible European tour began when the draw was made, putting us with Atletico Madrid, Widzew Lodz and Steaua Bucharest in Group B of the Champions League. In some ways I was sorry we hadn't made it into Group A along with Rangers because that would have been a bit interesting for me.

I have to say the news was greeted in a pretty low-key way in Dortmund, and I seemed to be about the only one who was a bit excited at the prospects. The rest of the lads had such a belief in themselves that they realised they would take care of each individual challenge when it came along. But I was the new kid on the block and the thought of the Champions League certainly stirred me up a bit.

The closer the opening game against Widzew Lodz at the Westfalen Stadium came, the more excited I grew. It clearly did mean that little bit more than usual to the club, a fact which was confirmed by signs of change in our usually well-ordered existence. Prior to games in the Bundesliga, for instance, we always stayed in the same hotel, but before European ties we moved to a different one. Even a minor thing like that made me realise it was big-time even to Borussia.

I don't know why, but it was at the start of that campaign that I developed all sorts of superstitions that have remained with me ever since. I always go to bed on the night before a match at midnight, for example, and I have to be up again before nine o'clock the following morning. On the Friday night I have to have steak for dinner, followed by ice-cream and chocolate sauce, all accompanied by fizzy water and apple juice.

On the morning of the game I have to have two bread rolls, one with cheese and the other without, plus some orange juice. And if it's an afternoon match I have to have a banana at 2.15 p.m. and if it's an evening kick-off I have it about three-quarters of an hour before the start.

It's all a bit silly, I suppose, but you get into such a habit that it's difficult to break, and that's particularly the case when you're doing well. But I'm not alone in having routines. All sorts of players stick by a tried and trusted pre-match schedule and even clubs tend not to change things either. Borussia always wanted us on the team coach at 10.45 a.m., and you didn't need to be told because it never changed when you were going training.

Indeed, during that Champions League run – and probably still now back at my old club – they stuck rigidly to preparations that worked well for everyone. The day before a European tie we would watch a video of the opposition and coach Ottmar Hitzfeld would make a few general points before we had dinner and a quiet night.

I roomed more often than not with Knut Reinhardt, a powerful left-back who had an explosive shot not unlike that of Jorg Albertz of Rangers. We would watch a bit of television and have a chat before trying to get a good night's sleep.

On the day of the game we left at precisely 10.45 a.m. for a light training session, before returning for a spaghetti lunch. It was always spaghetti. A few more hours in your bed was followed by a team meeting at 5.30 p.m., when we were told the line-up.

Ottmar always listed the team on a flip chart by their squad numbers. He would put up number one for Klos, 15 for Kohler – and I would hope to see 14, which was mine. Strangely, he would then list the opposition by their names. All the talk, of course, was done in German but if he had a specific point for me he would make it in English, and his co-trainer Michael Henke and goalkeeping coach Toni Schumacher also spoke English, so I could never go far wrong.

Anyway, we always played the same way regardless of

the opposition, and even though we were going a bit into the unknown against Lodz, we were more concerned with what we did.

The stadium was about 15 minutes from the team hotel and on the way all you could see was the black and yellow of Dortmund fans. You start to feel it then, and when you see the Champions League stars – the tournament logo – you really know you are in for a big Euro night. That's how it was before Lodz and I was buzzing at the prospect. Unfortunately, it all went horribly wrong for me on that opening night because I only lasted 25 minutes before being stretchered off.

That was bad enough, but it could certainly have been worse, because I injured myself making a tackle right on the edge of our penalty area. I actually thought it was a spot-kick but happily it wasn't. If it had been and Dortmund had gone on to lose the match because of it, who knows how things would have turned out?

Instead I got away with it, and although I didn't really think that was much consolation as I lay on the stretcher listening to the supporters chanting my name, I can look back now and accept I was a bit lucky.

In the event, I was replaced by Wolfgang Feiersinger. Heiko Herrlich scored twice and, although they pulled a goal back through Marek Citko late on, we won the three points that put us on the right road. Madrid, the other fancied team in the section, beat Steaua 4–0 that night so the two favourites to go through were off and running. It was all pretty satisfactory, even if I was forced to watch it from the bench.

Afterwards, Ottmar shook everyone's hand and the players went back across the pitch to the restaurant where the wives and families were waiting. Monica and Christopher were at the game and after I picked them up we headed home to Kruckel, which was only a ten-minute drive.

The following morning I went to hospital for a scan on

my knee, but it wasn't too bad. I had bruised ligaments that kept me out of the league game against Stuttgart the following Saturday but it could have been much worse.

And that was my Champions League début – short and not so sweet from a personal point of view. I didn't even swap jerseys with any of the Polish players because I wanted to hang on to my first one at that level.

Our second fixture was away to Steaua and I have to say that I didn't particularly like Bucharest, or at least what we saw of the city. Everything seemed so grey and dirty and for some reason it always seemed to be dark.

I remember Andy Möller and me sitting on the coach going to the stadium to train the night before the match. Andy spotted a guy sitting naked in a manhole, and when we returned to the hotel he was still there. He didn't look as if he had moved. People were clearly very poor and it was a sobering experience – especially as we stayed at an American-owned hotel that was spectacular.

The game was fairly straightforward for us but there was a surprise for me beforehand when I bumped into former Scottish referee Kenny Hope, who was there as a UEFA observer. England's Paul Durkin was the referee.

We won 3–0 with goals from Lars Ricken, a bizarre one from Jorg Heinrich after their goalkeeper had hit the ball off his shin, and Stephane Chapuisat and then we flew home with the job well done. With Atletico winning easily in Poland, we knew then that our meeting with the Spaniards at their Vicente Calderon Stadium next time round was going to be hugely significant. And so it was.

If anyone had doubted the importance of the Champions League before our Lauda Air flight touched down in Madrid, they were quickly shown otherwise for the place was teeming with media people. I escaped relatively lightly, but bigger names like Julio Cesar and Andy Möller were pounced upon to give their views.

Our build-up, predictably, was the same as usual but we were all delighted at the state of the pitch. It was like a bowling green, so there could be no excuses on that front. But if we were pleased about that then we weren't so taken on the way to the game when we 'enjoyed' our first encounter with the Atletico fans. They were mental and, worse still, looked positively evil. Lots of them had handkerchiefs over the lower part of their faces, others had scarves covering their mouths and noses, and they all made gestures at us. It was very hostile.

As for the match, I was up against Pantic, a very talented Yugoslav, while alongside me Michael Zorc was marking Czech star Radek Bejbl. We knew from Ottmar's talk that we had very important roles that night.

Everything went well, as it turned out, and Pantic didn't do too much. I hit the post after a shot from Julio had rebounded from their defensive wall and we won 1–0 thanks to a Stefan Reuter goal just after half-time. It was one hell of a result and they weren't best pleased. Simeone in particular was a bit upset, but that might have had something to do with the fact that I caught him on the chest with my studs during the game! He was so furious that he lifted up his shirt to show the referee the impression I had made on him and was promptly booked.

It didn't seem a very good idea to ask for Simeone's jersey in the circumstances, and besides, I wanted the one Pantic had been wearing. I didn't get it, though, and instead swapped with Antonio Toni.

We had back-to-back meetings with Atletico and the second was, for sure, a bit different. In all kinds of ways. It was a seriously hard game to play in because they were clearly still smarting from the defeat in front of a big home crowd, and that was especially the case with Pantic.

He was magnificent that night. He was wearing the number ten shirt I have always associated with great players and he wore it well. I remember he nutmegged me at one point – put the ball through my legs – and I had to pay to get back into the ground after another superb bit of skill.

He wanted to swap jerseys with me afterwards and I'm still convinced it was so he could put it in his pocket, where I had been for most of the evening!

We started well enough in that game, with Herrlich scoring early on, but Luis Roberto equalised and then Pantic got the winner from a free-kick. It was all a lesson to me, certainly, but fortunately the end result didn't do us too much damage because of our victory at their place earlier in the competition.

Next up was a trip to Poland and results throughout the group meant that we needed just a point to qualify for the quarter-finals. It's sometimes hard to go to these countries simply because they're so different from Germany or Scotland. I don't mean any disrespect but hotels are sometimes not as good and, more importantly, the actual pitches sometimes aren't as well looked after.

But I shouldn't complain about Lodz because I actually opened the scoring. Herrlich set me up and I sent a decent shot past their keeper from about 16 yards. It was a great feeling to get a goal, and particularly a Champions League one. Having said that, though, the Poles equalised inside a minute through Jacek Dembinski and the same player put them ahead just a few minutes later to put us under the cosh a bit. In fact, we struggled a little for a while before Kohler levelled it again on the hour.

And that was that. There were no wild celebrations or anything. Just quiet satisfaction at a job well done in the main. Anyway, we had one more match to play in the qualifying section and, believe me, when we thought of the money at stake we reckoned it was still pretty important!

That match, of course, was at home to Steaua and even though neither team had anything really to play for apart from pride and cash – or maybe because of that! – it was a remarkable match. The first thing I remember about the night was that Scotland's Hugh Dallas was the referee and Kenny Clark was the fourth official.

Not that it helped much to have countrymen as officials,

because within a few minutes Matthias Sammer was on to me to have a word with Hugh after a couple of decisions went against us! I'm not sure what the big man expected me to do about it, but clearly he felt I should have some influence. In fact, that was the start of a whole night of stick from the lads who weren't particularly impressed with my fellow Scot. There was maybe some excuse for Hugh, though, because like the rest of us he must have been nearly frozen solid that night. It was frighteningly cold in Dortmund.

Still, there was plenty of entertainment as we won 5–3. Chapuisat got a couple and Rene Tretschok, Riedle and Zorc scored our others, while Steaua's goals came from Adrian Ilie with a penalty, Marius-Achim Baciu and Aurel Calin. It was nothing if not interesting and we duly finished second in the group to Atletico Madrid on goal difference. That actually turned out to be a good thing for us because it meant we faced Auxerre rather than Ajax in the quarters, and after hearing from home how the Dutch side had beaten Rangers home and away I knew that that was a good thing.

We had finished with 13 points and, it has to be said, a lot of money. We were on vast sums – to me at least – for victories, and then a bumper bonus for making it through to the quarter-finals. It was a big thing financially and although the other lads might have been used to it I have to say I had never been involved in the kind of money we're talking about here.

In fact, the whole thing was like a dream come true. I was getting paid very, very well, but – and this was important to me – I was also a regular in a tremendous team and a few people had sat up and taken notice of my performances. That was very satisfying.

Equally so was the fact that I felt well and truly accepted by players like Sousa, Möller, Riedle and Kohler. I used to play Andy at head-tennis and we became pretty friendly. I swapped a Scotland top for a German one with him and we still keep in touch. It was the same with Paulo and even though he's now in Milan we still speak occasionally. They were good friends to me in Dortmund.

After all the drama of the group games it was probably just as well that we headed into the winter break, and we stopped for a few weeks believing we had done quite well to avoid the prospect of Ajax when things picked up again in March. Apart from the fact that they were an excellent side with players like Danny Blind, Ronald and Frank de Boer, Winston Bogarde, Patrick Kluivert, Marc Overmars and Jari Litmanen, they had also knocked Borussia out the previous season in the quarter-finals.

Equally, however, Auxerre had topped a strong section and when the time came we made sure we treated them with the respect they clearly deserved. We were back to the situation where away goals mattered, so it was important for us to do well in the first game at home. We went on to win 3–1 and played well on our way to that victory.

Riedle opened the scoring quite early on and after the interval Rene Schneider added a second, which we were very happy about. Unfortunately, Sabri Lamouchi pulled a goal back for the French before Möller added a vital third for us quite late on.

It was all pretty satisfying and gave us a good lead to take to France. But at the Stade Abbe Deschamps it was a different picture. In fact, it was one of the hardest games I've ever played in. The ground is quite small and tight and the atmosphere was tremendous as Auxerre battled to get back into the tie.

They were, indeed, a really good team and they put us through it a bit. We had to withstand a lot of pressure although, to be fair, we were good at that, and when Ricken scored midway through the second half we knew we were through.

Even so, their manager Guy Roux didn't believe it was all over and when we messed about a bit after the ball had gone out of play he wasn't best pleased. He's a real charac-ter and a legend in Auxerre, and he didn't take too kindly to trying to get the ball back himself from Matthias Sammer and Stefan Klos.

And that was us in the semi-finals of the European Cup where we knew, after their victory over Porto, Manchester United lay in wait. Being British, I knew more about the Old Trafford club than others, but I have to say that the German lads weren't particularly impressed with United's tremendous history and reputation. And why should they have been? Let's face it, most of the Borussia lads had seen and done more than any of the United players.

But there is a terrible arrogance about the English media when it comes to United in Europe. It infuriated me at the time and even looking back at it now it still does. I just couldn't believe the lack of respect shown to the Dortmund players, who were among the best in the world. It was staggering. I remember one reporter from Sky saying that at the time we were fourth in the Bundesliga when, in fact, we were second, and it was little inaccuracies like that that really riled me, because it was clear the media at least didn't rate Borussia.

There was also the widely held view in England that because United had beaten Porto 4-0 on aggregate in the quarter-finals we really shouldn't have been allowed on the same pitch. I recall another writer asking me in a kind of awestruck voice what the Dortmund lads thought of Roy Keane. I told him to go and ask them for himself but, to be honest, not all that many knew anything about him. They were clearly meant to but the bottom line is that the only United player the German lads were really knowledgeable about was Eric Cantona.

All these things annoyed me, and the closer we got to the game the more wound up I became. The final insult was when the media made a huge deal out of the fact that Peter Schmeichel was missing from the United side, happily ignoring the fact that we were without three key players of our own in Jurgen Kohler, Matthias Sammer and Julio Cesar!

When the talking stopped and the action got under way

I was bursting to ram a few words down a few throats, and we should have been well ahead at half-time, we were so much in command. Eventually we scored through Tretschok, and it was an interesting game. I had one small altercation with Nicky Butt when Keane added his tuppence worth, but at the end we were reasonably satisfied with a 1-0 lead to take to England. We felt that United, on the other hand, believed they had cracked it going home just a goal down.

What British clubs have failed to recognise, though – and I appreciate that this is a bit of a generalisation – is that continental teams are far better equipped than they are to score away from home. The old situation when a 1-0 defeat wouldn't have been too bad has gone. You need an away goal in Europe these days and we were perfectly comfortable in the belief that we would get one at Old Trafford.

I don't know whether or not Borussia thought it was an omen or whether it was simply the best place to stay when we were in Manchester, but the club chose the same hotel – Mottram Hall – that Germany used at Euro '96, and, let's face it, it didn't do them too much harm then.

It was a good time for me because I was staying on after the United match to meet up with Scotland for games against Austria and Estonia, and, of course, it was nice to be back in Britain. The only cloud on the horizon was the absence of Jurgen Kohler, but he arrived later and I was delighted to see him.

Borussia had so many top-class players, but Jurgen was unquestionably one of the best. He was a football god in Dortmund and when I played alongside him I could see exactly why. He was special and it gave us a big pre-match boost to have him available. It didn't take long, either, for him to make his mark because Eric Cantona had a fairly simple chance but somehow the ball came off Jurgen's studs and stayed out. Maybe when you're as good as Kohler is you carry a bit of luck as well, but I reckon he deserved it. Mind you, I would!

There was a terrific atmosphere at Old Trafford and a corner of the stadium was filled with black and yellow. It didn't take us long to give them something to sing about, either, with Lars Ricken scoring very early on. That was that, and we knew it even if United didn't.

To be honest, they could still be playing and they wouldn't have scored against us, but that was always our game plan and it worked to perfection. There must have been a lot of tears in Manchester that night because United felt they had been within touching distance of the trophy that is their Holy Grail.

In the end, though, they simply weren't good enough, despite what all the pundits had been saying – and when I say that I'm not demeaning them. It's a simple fact that Borussia were the better side, and if we had played them a few times rather than just twice we would have confirmed that. It might not make pleasant reading for the English, but if they had really done their homework on the German champions, they would have seen the evidence for themselves beforehand. There was certainly never any doubt in my mind what the outcome would be.

The result generally gave us all enormous satisfaction, and the fact that we had turned United over pretty comprehensively seemed the perfect answer to those who had suggested beforehand that Fergie's side were as good as through.

Instead, it was us who were in the European Cup final and Martin Kree, Andy Möller and I led the charge towards our fans at the end. They had been brilliant and we reckoned we had done them proud. It was a magic moment when we took our bow. Even the German lads showed some genuine excitement about our achievement, and when you think of what many of them had done in their careers, that says something. The guys were actually ecstatic, and the champagne flowed in the dressing-room. It was one of those evenings you wish would never end and which, unless you're very fortunate, come along only once in a lifetime.

One more thing added to the drama and excitement, because by then we knew who we would be facing in Munich, and the fact that it was mighty Juventus was the icing on the cake.

That night was also the first time I met German international manager Berti Vogts. He came into our dressing-room after the match and congratulated us all and I also bumped into snooker star Stephen Hendry, who seemed pleased to see me. The strange thing is I never did see Alex Ferguson. It was just one of those things. Our paths never crossed, but I imagine he must have been as dejected as I was delighted. It was a sore night for him and United.

Monica had come over for the match and my mum and dad were down from Scotland, so I think it's safe to say we had a wee party that night. The events of the following morning certainly sobered me up pretty quickly, though. I was driving a hired car to go back north and was struggling to find my way out of Manchester. That's my excuse for not wearing my seatbelt, for being on the mobile phone and for not having a child's car seat for Christopher when I was pulled over by the local constabulary.

Maybe not unnaturally, he asked me what I was doing, where I had been and so on. I happened to mention that I was on my way back to Scotland after playing football the previous night. Now, if he had been a Manchester United supporter I was in trouble – big trouble. Goodness knows what he might have thrown at me. As it turned out, I reckon he must have been a City man delighted he wouldn't have to listen to his pals crowing about how they were in the European Cup final. Honestly, it's the only explanation I can come up with, and I went on my merry way a happy and relieved man that the greatest 24 hours of my football life hadn't ended up with a court appearance.

5

A WINNER IN EUROPE

Dateline: Wednesday, 28 May 1997. Place: Munich. The greatest day of my football life. A day when I picked up a European Cup winners' medal, two Rolex watches, a considerable amount of money and enough memories to last me a lifetime. Not bad for a wee boy from Linwood.

Whatever I had done up till then paled into insignificance and, indeed, despite one or two achievements since, I have to say I can't imagine anything in the game can get any better than that.

It was a once-in-a-lifetime experience that not many Scots have enjoyed, and to say I am hugely proud of having been part of the Borussia Dortmund team that beat Juventus 3–1 in the Olympic Stadium doesn't begin to describe it.

Even now, some time on, the whole occasion is etched in my mind, from the minute on the Friday night nearly five days before when I discovered I was playing to the last moments of the huge non-stop party three days afterwards.

Once we had despatched Manchester United into oblivion the final was, of course, just about the only subject of conversation in and around Dortmund, where the people certainly like their football. There was a terrific buzz about the city in the build-up to the big game and I think everyone was caught up in it in some way or another.

Yet I have to say that Borussia is such a professional club that management and players worked hard at focusing on the usual day-to-day routine and, for that matter, the question of Bundesliga matches that had to be taken care of. Our last one before we headed for Munich was against Hamburg and on the Friday night there was a knock on the door of the room I was sharing with Knut Reinhardt. In walked Ottmar Hitzfeld to tell me I wasn't playing the next day.

It was a bit of a blow because I wanted to play every game. That must have registered on my face, because he went on to say I could play if I really wanted to, but that he would prefer it if I didn't so that I was 100 per cent for the following Wednesday. That certainly made the disappointment easier to accept!

Even so, I eventually made it on against Hamburg for the last 20 minutes, although we ended up losing 2–1. It was a strange game, because normally the Borussia lads would take a defeat very badly, always considering it a dent to their professionalism, yet that day I remember Jurgen Kohler telling me to forget the result and think of Juventus. 'That's all that matters,' he insisted. Believe me, that was unusual.

Other than that, the weekend and even the Monday passed as normal, with training along the usual lines. It was Tuesday, really, before we felt the whole thing was upon us. By then I had sorted out the 80 tickets we were allowed to buy. Some went to family, because a fair number came over from Scotland as you might expect. There were probably around 20 relatives at the game. Other tickets went to friends and neighbours in Dortmund.

So the scene was set, and when we left for the short flight to Munich there was a tremendous sense of expectation among the group. At the same time, I think everyone felt a bit for guys like Julio Cesar, Steffen Freund and Rene Schneider, who were all injured and who were travelling to watch the game the following day. It must be desperately disappointing to miss out on something like that.

We trained at the Olympic Stadium on the Tuesday night and I think every one of us had a fair idea then about what the team would be. There were often little signs of the way the coach was thinking and from a purely personal point of view my own place was confirmed when he pulled me aside and told me to play diagonal passes every time I had the chance. The instruction was music to my ears.

But once more I felt for a team-mate and this time it was Reinhardt, my room-mate, because he knew he wasn't even going to make it on to the bench for the biggest night in the club's history. There's not a lot you can say to guys in these circumstances, so players tend just to get on with it.

Even so, it was only after a light training session on the day of the match that the team was officially named by Hitzfeld, and he took the opportunity at that time to impress on me once again the need to play a diagonal pass whenever possible, because he felt Juventus could be caught a bit square at the back.

Throughout all the build-up – and considering the occasion it was – I felt remarkably calm. I accepted best wishes from lads like Rab McKinnon and Billy Davies as if it was an everyday occurrence.

Then it all went pear-shaped. On the way to the team bus I met the club's jack-of-all-trades – a wee guy called Manny who looked after the players – and he was all over the place. All he could mutter was: 'Nervous, nervous.' Well, that set me off. Up until then there hadn't been a problem. At that point I lost it. And it wasn't helped one little bit when I took my seat on the coach opposite Stefan Klos and looked across to see our goalkeeper a bag of nerves as well!

The journey to the Olympic Stadium took around half an hour and all along the route the streets were a sea of our yellow and black and the black and white of Juventus. It was an incredible sight.

The full impact of what I was involved in didn't actually hit me until I walked into the stadium. I had played there before against Bayern Munich but, by any stretch of the imagination, this was going to be a bit different and the enormity of it all hit me then.

There was an orchestra playing, the fans were singing, the big Champions League banner was lying in the middle of the pitch and my stomach was churning. Yet I can honestly say that in amongst the nerves there was no fear. I knew we were playing what many people considered to be the best club side in the world and that players like Didier Deschamps, Vladimir Jugovic, Christian Vieri, Zinedine Zidane and Alen Boksic were all household names. But I reasoned that Borussia had great players of their own and that I had come to understand that fully during the season. Respect for Juve, obviously; fear, definitely not.

I think we were all the same. The dressing-room was very quiet as the players went through their individual pre-match routines and then we all held hands – players, coaches, everyone – in a gesture of solidarity before we walked out to face our destiny.

The one thing I remember most of all in amongst the preliminaries to the main event was walking down the tunnel alongside the Juve players and spotting something I couldn't believe on Angelo di Livio's wrist. He had actually written down a scoreline, which I found strange enough, but when I looked again and read 3–0 – obviously in favour of Juventus – I couldn't catch my breath. I was staggered that any professional would do something like that and obviously want it to be seen into the bargain. I mentioned it quietly to Paulo Sousa, and although he told me that the Italian always did that before a big game, it still rankled a bit.

A nicer touch was when we walked out hand in hand with some Juventus youngsters. I don't know about them, but I was taken aback by the wall of sound we hit when we emerged into the stadium proper. The fans were incredible and to top it all off the Champions League anthem was being played at full blast.

I took one last look around at the whole thing and decided again that we had every chance when I saw the quality surrounding me. How could you fear for the 90 minutes ahead when you had Kohler, Sammer, Reuter, Möller, Riedle, etc. in your team? Mind you, that belief took a bit of a battering in the early stages of the game because the Italians grabbed it by the scruff of the neck. Christian Vieri had a very good early chance that went into the side netting, and I thought: here we go.

Gradually, though, we began to play and we began to rattle Juve. So it was no surprise when we opened the scoring after 29 minutes through Karl-Heinz Riedle. I'm just glad I played a part in the goal. It came after Angelo Peruzzi punched out an Andy Möller corner. The ball landed with me and I immediately sent it to the back post, where Karl-Heinz took it on his chest and then sent it back past Peruzzi. It was a glorious moment.

Our second goal followed quickly, as we dominated for a while. Another Möller corner caused mayhem in the Juve box and this time Riedle beat Peruzzi with a good header to give us an incredible 2–0 half-time lead which certainly wasn't in the script – at least according to di Livio.

Everything had gone so well generally in those first 45 minutes that coach Ottmar Hitzfeld kept things brief during the interval. He simply told us that we had another 45 minutes left in which we could make history and that was about it. We knew by then that we were within touching distance, but we also realised that we had some more hard work ahead and that was confirmed when we saw that Juve had brought Alessandro del Piero on for Sergio Porrini at the start of the second half. Del Piero is a terrific player and we knew he would be hungry to get into the action after being left out of the starting line-up.

That's exactly how it turned out, because he was on fire and proved it when he pulled a goal back for Juve after 64 minutes. It was not a good moment. I simply thought to myself that it couldn't be happening, because I knew the lift they would get from the goal and, equally, I wondered how it would affect us.

Hitzfeld, however, is an astute coach and he recognised the danger signs. Almost immediately he put Heiko Herrlich on for Riedle and then just after that replaced Stephane Chapuisat with Lars Ricken. It was, to say the least, inspired, particularly in the case of Ricken, who promptly made it 3–1 with a classic goal from his first touch after he moved on to a Möller pass.

As we were celebrating, I took a quick glance over at Zinedine Zidane and the look on his face said it all. I knew there and then there was no way back for Juventus and that it was all over bar the shouting.

The Italians generally must have realised that as well, because they started putting it about a bit. Paulo Sousa was done by a bad tackle and one of the Juve players spat on Matthias Sammer's face, which is one of the worst things you can do to a fellow professional. The big man, though, merely dismissed it in the manner of someone who had done his job and knew he was a winner.

We all were. When the final whistle went it was music to my ears, the best sound I've ever heard, and I just fell on my back in relief, joy, ecstasy, delight – call it what you like. It was an incredible feeling. We then just jumped on each other like big kids, and in amongst that managed to find time to shake the hands of the Juventus players before we were on our way once more to share the moment with the fans.

The Dortmund lads wanted their families to be involved as well and when I ran over to where Monica and Christopher were the only sound I could hear above the

I don't know how I was talked into having this one in the book. The less said about it the better

I've never forgiven my mum for that haircut

Former St Mirren star Jackie Copland presents me with a prize early on in my career. In case it's not immediately obvious, I'm on the far left

Fraser Wishart and Kenny McDowall, who is now a coach at Celtic, help me celebrate my 21st birthday

In among the big boys – Celtic's John Collins and Saints team-mates Thomas Stickroth and Victor

Happy to be a Saint – at that point, at least

ABOVE: A goal against Rangers and I join Tommy Coyne and Dougie Arnott –
together with the Motherwell fans – in the celebrations

BELOW: In action with Paul Kane of St Johnstone, then of Aberdeen

ABOVE: Little did I know when I slid in on Borussia Dortmund's Andy Möller
that he would later become a team-mate
(© Jeff Holmes of Scottish News & Sport)

BELOW: Praying for a move to Dortmund? No, just another missed chance as
Dougie Arnott throws up his arm in despair and Julio Cesar walks away a
relieved man

Now it's the other end in the European tie and this time I get it right as I clear off the line, watched by (from left to right) Lars Ricken, Rab McKinnon, Stephane Chapuisat, Chris McCart, Stevie Woods and Michael Zorc

One against one. Rangers' Charlie Miller and I tangle, while Tommy Coyne and Dave McPherson keep an eye on things

ABOVE: My name in lights at the Westfalen Stadium with the Borussia Dortmund fans in the packed south tribune below. I've made it at last

RIGHT: The greatest moment of my career, as I sit in the Olympic Stadium dressing-room with the European Cup for company
(© Matthias Hubert)

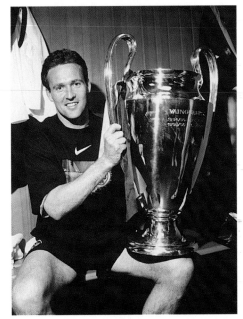

The scenes in the dressing-room after Borussia
Dortmund's glorious European Cup
final victory over Juventus:
ABOVE: I look on as Andy Möller, Paulo Sousa
and Jurgen Kohler enjoy the success
RIGHT: Bath-time, and instead of a rubber duck,
Jorg Heinrich and I have the Cup!
BELOW: This time Heiko Herrlich and I share the
moment of magic

rest of the din was the wee man crying! He was a bit frightened by everything going on around him but, remember, he was only two years old at the time!

Back down on the pitch it was bedlam, and it was an age before everything was sorted out for the presentation. Normally it would have been captain Matthias Sammer who collected the trophy but Michael Zorc had been our usual skipper, and even though he had had only two minutes of the action when he went on for Möller, it was he who was pushed up to collect the cup. I thought it was a great gesture by Sammer. We all received our medals ahead of the cup presentation, and then when Michael picked up the cup all you could hear was 'We are the champions' blaring out of the Olympic Stadium tannoy system.

It was an incredible feeling when we paraded the trophy in front of the fans and, not surprisingly, we all milked the moment for all it was worth. Afterwards, in the relative calm of the dressing-room, we had a visit from one or two of the Juve players, who congratulated us. We all appreciated that, because it was a hard time to be magnanimous.

Talking of time, it was there and then that Paulo Sousa and Karl-Heinz Riedle threw me their watches. It was the end of a bet we had that if we won the Bundesliga or the European Cup they would give me their watches. Actually, it wasn't really a bet because I didn't offer anything in return! Anyway, when I looked at the two Rolexes, I really did think all my Christmases had come at once. I think it was really just a gesture from the lads to show that I was one of them rather than anything to do with a bet, but whatever the reasons it was brilliant of them.

German boss Berti Vogts came in to add his congratulations as well and there was another familiar face around when I looked up at the door. It belonged to Dr Stewart Hillis of the Scottish Football Association, who was there in his UEFA capacity, and he shouted to me to get Andy Möller out for the compulsory drugs test.

'Aye, right,' I said, and promptly went back to the

celebrations. Imagine me trying to disentangle Möller from the mayhem and tell him he had to take a drugs test!

We did eventually leave the Olympic Stadium but even with my two new watches and my old one I couldn't tell you what time it was. All I know is that the music on the team bus was up full blast and you couldn't hear yourself think.

When we got back to the hotel where the families were I found Christopher half-asleep, but he was still cute enough to want the medal around his neck – and that's precisely where it went as I disappeared with the rest of the lads to get on with the festivities. The rest of the evening is a bit of a blur, but I enjoyed it all the same . . .

The following day we flew back from Munich to Dortmund, although even that simple task became a bit more complicated when there was a bomb scare with our aircraft. I don't know if it was an irate Juve fan or what, but for someone like me who doesn't really like flying in the first place – and who was suffering a bit anyway – it wasn't the news I wanted to hear.

We were actually on the plane and then told to get off it again. Then we were told the players could go but the wives and families couldn't. That seemed to provide the best answer, but when we got on again we discovered some of the players' families were on and some had been left behind. Monica and Christopher, for instance, weren't with us and I mentioned the fact to Paulo Sousa, who immediately demanded that the situation should be the same for everyone.

Once more the families were brought back on, although it was a nightmare from start to finish because Christopher cried from that moment to the moment we touched down in Dortmund. And when I say he cried, I mean he bawled. You wouldn't believe a youngster could have lungs like that!

There were supporters everywhere when we landed but Jorg Heinrich mentioned to me that I hadn't seen anything yet, and he was right enough.

When we took the coach trip to the city there were something like half a million fans out and about on the way to the main square. It was a sea of yellow and black. People were up trees and lamp-posts, hanging out of windows and generally on every vantage point where they could get a glimpse of the team and the European Cup.

We still had one Bundesliga game to play but, unusually for the ultra-professional Borussia, that seemed to have been almost forgotten in the midst of the celebrations.

We arrived at Peace Place, where we signed a book for the city, and then we were introduced to the fans one by one. We each had a turn at lifting the trophy and received a rapturous reception. It was almost too much to take in but a once-in-a-lifetime experience nevertheless, and the memories of that day will live with me forever.

Afterwards it was back to work and the prospect of Cologne at home, although we knew, too, that that would be a party day. Sure enough, a helicopter delivered the European Cup to the stadium and, led by guys like Kohler and Möller, we did a lap of honour and threw T-shirts into the crowd. The place was going crazy and the music was still blaring out of the tannoys five minutes after the game had started. Even after all that, we managed to win 2–1 which was good, because it would have been a horrible anti-climax if we had been beaten that day!

Scott Booth was actually over for that match, doing what I had done a year previously – trying to get himself a deal. Contrary to what some people might think, I had nothing to do with that move other than to give an opinion of Scott when I was asked by Ottmar Hitzfeld. Otherwise, it was down to him just as it had been down to me a year before. I do know, though, that he could hardly believe his eyes that day and if he had any doubts about wanting to go to Dortmund they were swept away there and then.

We partied again that night – surprise, surprise – and I'll never forgive Karl-Heinz Riedle for introducing me to two of life's vices then. He had me drinking grappa and smoking cigars! I had never done either before, so there was a certain novelty value involved. It's probably just as well that I wasn't too struck on grappa and it's not something that I've gone back to, although I must admit that any time I've won anything since I've kept up the old cigar routine.

I returned home the following day and, to be honest, I didn't need a plane. My head was in the clouds anyway. I was clutching a European Cup winners' medal, I was an awful lot better off financially, I had an engraved cup given to the players by Borussia, I had been on a stage that previously I had only dreamed of and, although I didn't know it at the time, I was only a few months from making that trip home permanent.

All sorts of thoughts ran through my head on that journey back to Glasgow, yet the overriding feeling I had was one of satisfaction. So many people had doubted my ability to play at the highest level with a club of Borussia Dortmund's stature, yet there I was with the most tangible reward from a wonderful season.

I had proved something to myself first and foremost. But I felt I had made a point to some other people as well and that was why I had a small smile of satisfaction on my face as I stepped back on to Scottish soil.

Germany was the making of me as a player and, for that matter, as a person.

6

HOMING IN ON GLORY

Football being the game it is, you tend to hear about things like transfers before they become in any way official news, and so it was with my proposed move back to Scotland and Celtic. It's the way of the world in this game of ours.

So it was when I was doing my pre-season training with Borussia Dortmund that I first heard of interest being expressed in me by Parkhead coach Wim Jansen and assistant Murdo MacLeod.

Coincidentally, around the same time I discovered that the club's general manager, Jock Brown, did not rate me as a player. A lot has happened since then, of course, but as the months have passed that initial suspicion has been reinforced by people I know and trust and, indeed, the whole subject was publicly aired at the worst possible time, when the Scotland squad was in France for the World Cup finals.

MacLeod went public with the news that I have known all along – he and Wim wanted me at the start of the

1997–98 season, but Brown didn't. I have to say that I was as disappointed then as I am now in the general manager's belief that I wasn't good enough for Celtic. I had just finished my best season in football by winning a European Cup winners' medal with Dortmund and I would have thought that that would have been pedigree enough to justify a return to Scottish football.

This game, though, is all about opinions and Brown is as entitled to one as anyone else. Fortunately, I was really only interested in those belonging to the people I believed mattered most – Jansen and MacLeod.

Even so, the doubts raised within Parkhead came close to snookering the move because at one stage I was so fed up hearing that people in a section of the club didn't fancy me that I told Celtic there was no way I was moving. And, believe me, that was hard to do because when I had first become aware of the interest I knew straightaway that I wanted to return to Scotland to go to Celtic.

It had been a fantastic year in Germany – a spell beyond my wildest dreams – and I would have stayed for the duration of my contract, another two years, but for the Celtic interest and a few domestic problems. The biggest single factor, undoubtedly, was my family. I loved being with my wife Monica and son Christopher, but if they were in any way unhappy then so was I. And we did have problems. Christopher had to spend a few days in hospital in Dortmund and it was very difficult for us to ensure he received the treatment we felt was proper. It all comes down to the language problem and although we had picked up quite a bit of German there was no way we could work our way around all the medical terms. It was hard for us to communicate.

Monica was unsettled by the difficulties in communicating and so was I. Christopher's problem is ongoing to an extent, and it was then that we first really spoke about the possibility of going home. There was another reason as well. We discovered around May that Monica was pregnant and, naturally, we were delighted. Unfortunately, though, she had a miscarriage. Indeed, I discovered the bad news just days before the Champions League final against Juventus and it was a bitter blow. The only good thing to emerge from it all was the fact that Monica was relatively okay, and that was a huge relief. But those were difficult days, and once again the fact that we weren't at home where she could be near family and friends at a terrible time convinced us we should think about a move.

So when I heard the first whispers about Celtic as I trained in Lucerne with Borussia, I was quite excited. I knew instantly that it was a club I would enjoy playing for. Remember, I had seen enough of the place and the fans to know it was special and I also knew that they were finally prepared to think on a really big scale after hearing for years about how they never spent money.

Celtic's interest and the family unrest came together with immaculate timing, although it didn't exactly all go the way I thought it would because it was several months down the line before the deal was finalised.

In between times I continued to do my best for Dortmund, and it wasn't until mid-October that Borussia informed me that Celtic had made their interest official with a bid I understood to be around £2 million. General manager Michael Meier and coach Nevio Scala both insisted they would rather I stayed in Germany, but the opportunity for me to return to a huge club like Celtic was overwhelming. I wanted to do it although, heaven knows, there were times even before I put pen to paper that I had second thoughts.

Some of those stemmed from the nagging doubts I had that a move could ever be completed because of Jock Brown's views. He was, after all, in control of transfers in and out of the club and I often wondered if Wim Jansen's insistence that I was a player he wanted could outweigh the general manager's opinion.

Then there was a phone call I received from Paolo Sousa,

my close pal at Dortmund, who told me his agent would have no trouble fixing me up with a transfer to Italy. That was flattering, obviously, but it was never an option I seriously considered.

The final thing that came closest of all to making me pull the plug on returning to Scotland happened, ironically, when the deal was virtually done and dusted. Unusually, Borussia and I agreed to make it public that I was leaving before our Champions League match against Parma at the Westfalen Stadium on 5 November 1997. I went on television, announced I was going and briefly gave the reasons behind the decision.

What I didn't expect, however, was the response the news evoked. I spoke to people at the club on the night of the match and asked them to make me up a banner thanking the fans for their support, little expecting the incredible scenes that took place. I walked out before the game with the banner and from that moment until the end of an unforgettable night the supporters simply never stopped chanting my name.

In the game itself, Andy Möller put us ahead and then we were awarded a penalty, which the fans demanded I take. But then, as now, I would never put personal glory before the team effort. That was one of the many things I really learned to appreciate in Germany. Möller took it instead and scored to give us a 2–0 victory and a nice send-off for me.

Even the result, mind you, seemed almost insignificant compared with what followed the final whistle. I immediately ran to the fans and applauded them before taking off my jersey and giving it to a young disabled fan. I did a lap of honour as the huge crowd stood and clapped me and all the while Nevio Scala and the players stood on the sidelines applauding as well. The tannoy blasted out the Celtic anthem 'You'll Never Walk Alone', and when I stood in the middle of the field taking my bow I kept spotting green and white scarves and jerseys in the crowd. It was an incredibly emotional moment, and it was really only then that I realised what I was leaving behind.

Put it this way: if I had had a mobile phone on me at that moment and Monica had phoned to say let's just stay, I wouldn't have had any hesitation. As it was, she was back in Scotland blubbing at the scenes she was watching on television. There were tears in my eyes as well, because I simply never expected a reaction like that from the Dortmund fans. I had always had a good relationship with them but I hadn't fully realised how good until then. It was really hard to take it all in.

It didn't get any easier in the dressing-room either, for the players – my team-mates for just a year – all joined up to thank me and wish me well. And it wasn't over even then. When I went upstairs at the club to sign my release form from Borussia, Michael Meier asked me one final time to reconsider. It wasn't really emotional blackmail, but considering the state I was in it felt a bit like it. Somehow I managed to say no.

When I finally left the stadium, knowing it was all over at Dortmund, I was a bit choked. I don't mind admitting it. It wasn't helped, either, by a big banner spread over my car wishing me good luck, nor by the gifts the fans gave me as I walked away sometime in the early hours of the morning.

People back in Scotland who happened to watch the scenes from the Westfalen Stadium on satellite television that night have often said to me how incredible it was, and I can only go along with that. It was, honestly, a very difficult – yet flattering – night for me.

And although some will find this hard to believe, there is no doubt in my mind that that evening in Dortmund contributed hugely to my poor form when I first joined Celtic. I simply found it hard to shrug off the emotion of that evening. I know some people have even said I didn't look happy when I was signing for Celtic, but that is nonsense. Everything happened so quickly around that time that I struggled to come to terms with it all, and I know I suffered.

Jock Brown, of all people, picked me up at the airport and took me on the rounds of the medical checks, which I have to say were pretty stringent. The general manager didn't, at any time, say anything to me about any reservations he had and instead chatted generally as I went about the business of proving I was fit enough at least! By then, of course, the financial side of things had been worked out in fine detail and I have to say that the package that brought me home nailed those biscuit-tin days. I was pretty well paid by Borussia and I can assure you I remained pretty well paid when I came back to Glasgow.

But I can honestly also say that in just about every career decision I have made it has been about football rather than money. I had a gut feeling that Celtic was perfect for me – despite the side issue – and by then the club had given some indication of their ambition by making a host of signings, including Craig Burley and Henrik Larsson. It all just seemed so right. I've already mentioned the club and the fans, but I also like a challenge and the prospect of going in against Rangers and trying to stop them winning ten titles in a row was an appealing one.

So I signed a four-year deal, trained on the Friday morning with my new team-mates and faced the media. I already knew a lot of the players from international duty with Scotland so it didn't take me long to feel part of things and in the afternoon we went to Cameron House Hotel at Loch Lomond to prepare for the Saturday match against . . . Rangers.

I didn't play well that day and we lost 1–0. I didn't play any better next time out against Motherwell either and I suppose Celtic fans were wondering exactly what they had bought. We did manage a draw against Rangers the following time, but I have to admit it was no real surprise to hear from Wim Jansen that I wouldn't be playing in the Coca-Cola Cup final against Dundee United.

I knew better than anyone that I wasn't delivering in those first few weeks and I couldn't possibly have any complaint about the coach's decision. He had to do what was best for the team, and certainly I simply wasn't playing well enough. So on to the substitutes' bench I went for the big occasion at Ibrox.

Looking back at it all now, I still believe what I thought at the time – namely that I was suffering from a Dortmund hangover. Not the drinking kind, I hasten to add, simply the fact that I couldn't shrug off the enormity of what had happened to me when I left Borussia.

It had been a huge mental thing to leave Germany in the midst of that kind of public acclaim and I had found the whole episode very draining. It's the only excuse I can offer for my poor early form at Celtic. I was fit, I was eager to do well and I was delighted to be back in Scotland. But it certainly took me longer than I expected to leave Borussia Dortmund behind.

My first few games for Celtic were, frankly, a nightmare. Happily, things improved beyond all recognition as the season went on and I ended up with a Coca-Cola Cup winners' medal – under false pretences, I admit – and a Premier League championship gong as well. I must say that neither seemed particularly likely in those dark early days at Parkhead, but all that proves, once more, is that nothing is certain in football.

Now I hope I can go on and collect more silverware with Celtic, even though I seem to have been linked particularly with Leeds United and Bayern Munich in recent months. That has certainly not been my doing but throughout the summer of 1998, when we had no head coach, it was inevitable that there would be rumours. Obviously, if all things are equal, I don't want to go anywhere.

I've dealt with how I see my future in more detail elsewhere in this book, so here I would rather look back on a roller-coaster season that started badly, faded, improved and ended in a blaze of glory. Talk about the big dipper. Celtic's year had an unbelievable number of ups and downs which seemed to take the players and fans from incredible highs to unbelievable lows with virtually nothing in between. I have never known a season like it. Of course, it all hinged on Celtic trying to stop Rangers winning a world-record ten titles in a row and the Ibrox club trying their level best to achieve that. Throw the hangovers from the season before into the pot and then add Hearts, because they had a tremendous season, and all the ingredients were always there for it to be a bit different.

I don't think, though, that anyone could have scripted the kind of championship battle that ultimately occurred. I can only talk about it from when I joined the club in November, but by then Celtic had recovered from the awful start that had seen us lose the opening two games to Hibs and Dunfermline. It was the worst start imaginable and, predictably, led to a chorus of discontent about Wim Jansen, who had taken over only a couple of weeks earlier. Every coach who takes over a club asks for time to sort things out, and it is a not unreasonable request that every-one nods sagely about.

Then, after two defeats for either of the two big Glasgow teams, there is a crisis. It's the way of the Old Firm. There is only black and white, never any grey. It's been the same in the city for more than a century, so don't expect me to try and change it. Better brains have tried and failed. Come to that, generally they're still trying – and failing – to change things.

Some people hate the Old Firm rivalry and all the things it stands for and I must admit I have no time for any kind of bigotry. I don't pretend to understand all the back-ground to it, and although some people won't like to hear this, I'm not particularly interested. Religion and politics are subjects to be avoided as far as I'm concerned and if that makes me sound stupid I'll just have to live with it. Priests, ministers and members of parliament are paid to sort things out in those areas. I'm paid to play football.

I have private views on different things but, aside from saying I'm no bigot, I don't plan to enter into any arguments about the great divide between the two Old Firm clubs.

Anyway, that has taken me off the subject. The point was we had an awful start, people were already calling for Jansen's head and Rangers' ten in a row looked as if it might happen even that early. Gradually, however, Celtic got their act together – I think helped by the confidence taken from two UEFA Cup draws with Liverpool – and by the time I arrived back in Glasgow the lads had reached the Coca-Cola Cup final and were back in business in the championship race.

After my début, when I went on as substitute against Rangers at Ibrox, we were three points behind Hearts and had been overtaken by our Old Firm rivals, who were two points clear of us. The situation, though, was a whole lot better than appeared likely after the first 180 minutes of league action.

I have documented my poor start earlier but in a blow-by-blow account of my Celtic season I can't, unfortunately, dismiss it here. I replaced Tom Boyd in that Ibrox match but, in my own defence, it was so late on that I couldn't do very much about it. Not that I was playing well enough anyway, but the thought was there! Richard Gough's goal was enough to give Rangers what seemed a priceless victory.

It was my first taste of the famous Glasgow derby and it was, well, interesting. I wasn't completely unaware of the fixture, of course, but imagine everything you hear about the match and then double it. The tempo of the game is very quick but the bottom line is that if you're good enough you can make time and space for yourself in any match.

The biggest problem that day was, naturally, the defeat. The players were very down after it but Wim Jansen was the same as he always was. It almost didn't matter whether you won, lost or drew – Wim only wanted to look forward to the next match. He always insisted you couldn't change what had happened and that there was nothing you could do about a game that was over, so you shouldn't dwell on it. It makes sense, really. It wasn't, however, the start I wanted and it even managed to get worse in the next game at Motherwell, when I was terrible. I couldn't do anything right. Regi Blinker was sent off, Mickey Weir and Owen Coyle scored for 'Well, I was substituted by Morten Wieghorst and we lost 2–0. It wasn't really going according to the script.

On to Rangers once more, and with two games coming up against Dundee United on successive weekends – in the league and the Coca-Cola Cup final – I was beginning to wonder if there were only ourselves, Rangers, Motherwell and United in the country!

I certainly found it easier to start that second Old Firm fixture than it had been to go on as a substitute in the first, and it was my first real experience of the famous huddle the players have before matches. I think it's a great idea. At Borussia we did something similar, but it was held in the dressing-room. Bayern Munich, though, did it out on the pitch like Celtic. It's simply a last chance to get the guys well and truly hyped up. Captain Tom Boyd delivers a few well-chosen words to gee everyone up and when we break away from the huddle the noise is unbelievable. That day it was frightening!

We knew it was another huge match – Old Firm games tend to be anyway – but after losing the last one we couldn't afford another defeat. It was dramatic as usual, and Paul Gascoigne was sent off for tangling with Morten. Even so, Rangers took the lead with ten men through Marco Negri and I think we all thought: oh, no, not again. Celtic hadn't won an Old Firm game for ages and to go one down in that one was a disaster. It also made it incredibly difficult because Rangers are hard to beat when you're level, never mind behind.

The huge crowd, though, lifted us and we equalised very late on through Alan Stubbs. We certainly deserved at least a point but there was a lot of relief about the place that we hadn't lost again. It meant we stayed three points behind Rangers, but it could have been worse.

Those Old Firm clashes hard on the heels of each other gave me some insights into the fixture and the hype that goes with it. I don't know if it's the same at Ibrox, but the build-up before the matches was generally quite low-key inside Celtic Park. Maybe that was down to Wim and his attitude, but most of the excitement and frenzy was coming from outside the club. You can't ignore it, of course, but you can keep it at a distance.

Anyway, with those two games out of the way we could concentrate on other things again, and that meant the two matches against United. The first was fairly straight-forward, although I had to go off with an ankle knock, and we won 4–0, which gave us a big psychological lift ahead of the final.

We went to Cameron House at Loch Lomond to prepare for the Ibrox meeting with United. It's great down there, although not the traditional place for Celtic, who always used to go to Seamill Hydro in Ayrshire.

This time, however, it wasn't a particularly happy hunting ground for me because on the morning of the game Wim pulled me aside before we boarded the coach and told me I wouldn't be playing. To be fair, it wasn't a huge surprise because I knew I wasn't performing well. And I had no complaints because the team must always come before any individual. Morten Wieghorst played and he was entitled to, because he had been doing well before I arrived.

I was on the bench and I watched the lads play brilliantly on their way to a 3–0 victory. I did get on in the last minute or so, but I think that was only Wim wanting me to get a touch because I didn't contribute anything.

Celtic were in the home dressing-room at Ibrox and I can't imagine it had heard before too many of the songs sung that day! It was a real boost for the club to get a trophy and, of course, terrific for Jansen to land one of the big prizes. The fans, naturally, were ecstatic but the players were just as delighted. Wim congratulated us all individually but didn't do much more than that. He's seen and done it all before, so he is happy to let players get on with it.

The only disappointment for me was actually on behalf of lads like Darren Jackson. He didn't even make the bench that day, yet I was there or thereabouts despite being just in the door.

But the spirit at Celtic Park is great and no one seemed to bother too much when the champagne was flowing back at our own ground. The celebrations were a bit odd for me because I was new and at the back of my mind I knew some outsiders still didn't think I wanted to be at the club, which couldn't have been further from the truth. I was delighted to be a Celtic player but that Dortmund send-off was proving a problem.

7

STOPPING TEN IN A ROW

My early form was a huge cloud hanging over me for a few weeks as I struggled to settle, and in fact it wasn't until the next game against Kilmarnock at Rugby Park that I felt I was getting back to something like the form I knew I was capable of. We drew 0-0 and I was booked for a foul on Alex Burke.

At least I felt a bit better about that personal performance but the real breakthrough in terms of my own form came the next week against Aberdeen at Pittodrie. It's always a big game up there even though they were struggling a bit at the time. We ended up winning comfortably by 2-0 and were never really in any danger. Darren and Henrik Larsson scored and I felt I did well – which was a long-overdue feeling. It's good to get a result up there at any time because, apart from anything else, it makes the long journey home seem a bit easier.

It was a good spell around then and we beat Hearts 1-0, courtesy of a great Craig Burley goal. Craig scored a lot of important goals for Celtic and it was good to see. I had only really ever seen him in the right wing-back role for Scotland, where he didn't get much opportunity to get goals, but he clearly revelled in the other position for the club and notched up some superb efforts.

That was another important victory because the Tynecastle team had surprised some people by staying there or thereabouts in the title race and even then there was no real indication, as some insisted, that their bubble was about to burst.

Next up was Hibs and the other half of the Edinburgh duo were dismissed easily. We certainly seemed to be on a roll. We were scoring freely and, just as importantly, we weren't giving much away.

Unfortunately, you always get a hiccup in those circumstances and, sure enough, we discovered the truth of that when we went to Perth to play St Johnstone. It shouldn't have been there that we faltered, in truth, because normally we would have beaten Saints, but that day we didn't play well and paid the price. It was just after Christmas and George O'Boyle gave us an unwanted present.

Then – surprise, surprise – it was back to Old Firm matters and after our good run that defeat against Saints certainly brought us back to earth with a crash. Wim always took note of the players' feelings and before the match against Rangers he asked us if we wanted to go away or stay at home. Perhaps bearing in mind the time of year, the lads opted to be with the families, although if there had been enough of the squad preferring to go to Cameron House or wherever, that's what we would have done. The majority rules in these situations.

Our stay-at-home theory certainly seemed to work because we were by far the better team on 2 January. It had been ten years since we'd won a Ne'erday fixture so a win was long overdue, and we delivered it to a delirious support.

Craig set us on our way with a great goal after a brilliant

pass from Jackie McNamara and we were all over them. They simply couldn't get out to get at us, and it was a terrific performance. We added a second goal when I scored and that was that. I'll be accused of milking the moment of my goal now, but I can't let it pass without some comment. I actually knew the moment I struck it that it was going in. It was just one of those efforts. It dropped nicely, I caught it perfectly and we were 2–0 up. It was a fantastic feeling.

Looking back at it now, I realise two things about that game. The first is obvious: how important it was for us to win. The second is less obvious, but matters to me. I needed a goal – and one against Rangers was even better – to convince everyone. I probably felt the same way Maurice Johnston did when he scored for Rangers against Celtic because he had a point to prove and he was accepted more by Ibrox fans after his Old Firm goal. It was a bit the same for me. Lots of things have happened since then, yet when I meet Celtic supporters it's still the first thing they want to talk about.

It was a very big win for us altogether and I remember Tosh McKinlay telling me that whoever won that New Year match went on to win the title. I also remember going on Sky Television afterwards and having to present champagne to man of the match Craig Burley. He wasted no time in exploding it back in the dressing-room.

It all reinforced my view that we could do it, but more than anything I was happy for the fans that day because they were due a victory over Rangers and it was a big hurdle for us all to have overcome.

But if my goal against Rangers was a good one, I have to say, in all modesty, that the one that followed against Motherwell was even better. I was on a goalscoring roll! Seriously, though, Fir Park is a difficult ground for visitors because the fans are right on top of you, and I should know. They clearly hadn't missed me when I returned! We wasted an opportunity when Darren Jackson missed a penalty but I scored with a great strike and a point wasn't that bad.

The Scottish Cup provided a welcome break and we disposed of Morton without too much difficulty before facing Dundee United once more. The one thing I had learned by then about Celtic – and, I presume, Rangers – was that you're expected to win every match. At St Mirren and Motherwell we often looked on away points as a bonus, but with the Old Firm it's different. Home or away, you're expected to deliver. So even though Tannadice is not an easy place to go to, we went in search of a win.

Sometimes you can do things in a bit of style; on other occasions you have to roll up your sleeves and battle. This 2-1 victory was courtesy of the latter. There was nothing pretty about it but it was vital nevertheless.

Aberdeen by then had appointed Alex Miller, so the latest fixture with them was always going to be more difficult than before. He gets sides well organised and they are difficult to beat, but Morten, Darren and Henrik scored in a 3-1 win. We were particularly pleased because we had to come from behind after a David Rowson deflected shot beat Jonathan Gould.

Hearts away was my first real introduction to the Bobby Tait Syndrome. We probably played our best football of the season that day and yet came away from Tynecastle with just a 1-1 draw. Jackie opened the scoring, and although we had numerous chances to add to that we failed. Even so, we felt as comfortable as you ever can when you're just one goal ahead, but what we didn't reckon on was several minutes of injury time.

As fate would have it, Hearts snatched an equaliser through Jose Quitongo deep into extra-time and we were gutted. No one knew where the vital minutes had come from and referee Tait was the talk of the steamie in the dressing-room. I was unaware of his alleged leanings towards Rangers but others clearly knew and we weren't too happy, to say the least. We were certainly contrasting figures to the Hearts lads. Tynecastle manager Jim Jefferies had done a dance of delight at the equaliser and they obviously realised they had been handed a 'get out of jail free' card.

It all left us with a bit of a sour taste in our mouths but, as Wim always insisted, we couldn't dwell on it and instead got it out of our system with a good cup victory over Dunfermline at East End Park. The notable thing about that tie was a goal from Harald Brattbakk, who had taken a bit of stick since his arrival from Rosenborg. I felt that was a bit unfair, because it always takes time to settle in a foreign country – and I should know.

Anyway, that goal helped Harald, and his next outing silenced more of the critics because he scored all four goals in our 4–0 victory over Kilmarnock. He and Henrik had an almost telepathic understanding in that match and all the lads were delighted for him.

He kept his run going with another two goals in the 5–1 victory over Dunfermline and then we dug deep to win 1–0 against Hibs in Edinburgh, when Marc Rieper scored. Alex McLeish had taken over by then and although he and I had had our fair share of disagreements at Fir Park we had a chat that day and it was fine.

I was glad we won that afternoon because I was going to a supporters' night out in Bathgate to collect Player of the Year and Young Player of the Year awards on behalf of Henrik and Simon Donnelly respectively, and it's nice to go with a victory behind you.

It was back to the cup after that and what a game we had against Dundee United. We were sick of the sight of each other, but it didn't prevent it from being a terrific tie. We eventually won it through an own goal from Erik Pedersen very late on, after Morten and Harald had scored for us and the impressive Kjell Olofsson had scored twice for them.

Incredibly, we then had them again in the league after that. To be honest, it is difficult to beat a team every time when you play them so often, so we had to settle for a 1–1 draw. We were caught by a bit of a sucker punch when Olofsson scored again.

There are times when the result is more important than the performance and we were at that stage when we beat Aberdeen 1–0, courtesy of a Burley penalty. We just wanted the three points. Nothing more, nothing less. It was getting to that time of the season.

Against Hearts, we had Bobby Tait as the man in the middle again. It was strange, really, because Stephane Mahe was stretchered off late on yet there was no injury time played. The score? It finished 0–0.

Old Firm fixtures are never far away in the Scottish set-up and the next one was the semi-final of the cup. I must admit I didn't feel up to it. I had had flu all week and felt terrible. I spoke to Murdo MacLeod and physio Brian Scott about it and I got tablets, but I struggled. I certainly wasn't 100 per cent when the time came, but I decided to take a chance and thought I could manage an hour at least. In the event that was all I could give, because although I stayed on for the whole 90 minutes I couldn't raise a canter after 60.

Funnily enough, the serious action was late on as Ally McCoist did what he's done to Celtic a few times over the years with a goal and Jorg Albertz seemed to finish it off. Craig scored what proved to be just a consolation goal for us, but our other consolation was that we felt if we had to lose one of the two vital matches that were left against Rangers, it was better that it happened in the cup than the league.

We had to bounce back regardless and we did that on a miserable night at Rugby Park when Simon Donnelly hit a magnificent winner. With time running out in the championship race, that was a huge victory. Our fans that night seemed to take over the place and that gave us a big lift.

Then it was the Ibrox club again, and whatever I said earlier about being better to lose in the cup than the league

– forget it. We lost that one as well. Jonas Thern scored a wonder goal and then Albertz continued his hot streak with a second. We were very, very disappointed but I think Wim came into his own at times like that. He never blasted individuals or put pressure on people. He instead consigned it to the history books, and you would never have guessed the title race was all back in the melting pot. He was the essence of calm and it rubbed off on us, even in amongst the disappointment.

That was the end of my Old Firm experiences for the season, but they had been nothing if not interesting. Rangers had a lot of good players, but for me three probably stood out for one reason or another. Andy Goram was a magnificent servant to the Ibrox club and I don't think anyone at Celtic Park will have been sorry to see him go. I can understand now what former Celts manager Tommy Burns meant when he said he would have Goram's name on his headstone with an inscription that went something like: 'He broke my heart.' Goram was unbelievable. Some of the saves he made against us were unreal. They shouldn't have been allowed. I hadn't fully appreciated just how good Andy was until I played against him for Celtic but he was as good as they get. He was special. You needed extra-special efforts – like mine in the Ne'erday game! – to beat him.

Brian Laudrup falls into a similar category and he did us a bit of damage in his time too. If he didn't play, Rangers tended to struggle a bit, and although I have huge admiration for the Dane, I must add that I thought Enrico Annoni played him brilliantly when they met.

So to Paul Gascoigne. He is, unquestionably, a great player and I have to say I was astonished when England left him out of their World Cup squad in the summer. It's obviously impossible to know for sure if he would have made any difference, but there is no doubting his ability to change games with a touch or two and it would have been interesting to see what might have happened in France.

I played against him a few times during the season and I cannot recall any particular problem I had – apart from a booking I picked up after a slight altercation in the New Year game! Gascoigne actually thought he was being shown the yellow card but, to be fair to him, when he realised it was me he told the referee that there was nothing in it and not to bother. It didn't make any difference, of course, but it was a nice gesture. In that same game, after I had scored our second, the next time we were close to each other he said 'Great goal', and not that many players would have done that.

He was, though, a bit of an enigma. He had a fiery temper when things weren't going his way and that was probably what caused our dust-up, because I had been told to man-mark him when he came on as a substitute in that match and he didn't like it. Yet, in saying that, there was no real malice about him. After we squared up to each other, it was forgotten in an instant when he was pleading on my behalf. He also had his moments of magic and when you think what he did for Rangers you would be hard pushed to argue about his worth. He was also good for Scottish football because it's fantastic to have players of that ability here. His talent will certainly be missed.

Back at the title race, Hibs beat Hearts on the weekend of the Old Firm meeting to finally end their challenge and that left Rangers and us on the same number of points – they had a better goal difference – with just four games left to play. People said we had the easier run-in but there's really no such thing and although I remained quite confident I know some of our fans lost their bottle! I can sympathise with them because they had suffered a lot in previous years and the prospect of losing out this time – with ten in a row and all the rest – must have been too much to bear.

Their worries couldn't exactly have been eased, either, when Stevie McMillan scored against us for Motherwell next time out. It was all we needed. But Craig and Simon scored twice apiece to ease the tension. Rangers had to go to Aberdeen the following day and I thought the Dons might get something from the game, although I was well pleased when it turned out to be a victory rather than just the draw I had anticipated. I didn't watch the match on television for the simple reason that I couldn't influence what happened, but it didn't stop me from having a quiet smile when I heard the 1–0 scoreline.

When we went back into training on the Monday there was a bit of a buzz about the place after the weekend results but Wim kept us focused. We knew we had a bit of a cushion at a good time, but he insisted we think about nothing other than the forthcoming match against Hibs. He was right, although in the end we could only draw at home to the Easter Road team and at the same time Rangers were beating Hearts at Tynecastle to prove that nothing was settled.

Then, the next weekend, Rangers lost to Kilmarnock, who were chasing a European place, and we had Dunfermline at East End Park on the Sunday. On the Saturday afternoon I took myself, Monica and Christopher off to a toy store near Celtic Park and refused to even listen to what was happening to the Ibrox lads. Then my desire to find out the score got the better of me. I switched on the car radio just as Ally Mitchell scored and I came close to ploughing straight over a roundabout!

We knew then that victory over the Fifers would mean it was all over. We would be four points clear with just one match left. There was a huge feeling of anticipation about Celtic Park, heightened by the fact that the club had organised big screens for a beam-back from East End Park. I really felt the pressure when I saw them. The hype was incredible and even as we were leaving for the match there were fans all over the place.

Simon Donnelly put us in front against Dunfermline and the supporters, who seemed to have taken over the ground, went wild. We were within touching distance. Tantalisingly close. But 1–0 is seldom a big enough lead to be comfortable with and we knew that. We were very conscious of needing another goal to make it safe.

There was another goal all right but it came at the wrong end. When I saw a header from substitute Craig Faulconbridge loop over Jonathan Gould into the net, I felt physically sick. I was drained. Gutted. Actually, the feeling was very similar to the one I felt when Alessandro del Piero scored for Juventus against Borussia Dortmund in the European Cup final. It was, you'll gather, a fairly awful moment.

So a 1–1 draw proved nothing and there was a massive feeling of anti-climax. We knew we had blown one opportunity, yet strangely that gave us the belief that we would not do so again on the last day of the season against St Johnstone.

It was, one way and another, an eventful week. Monica and I were expecting our second child, so when the lads all went out for a Chinese meal on the Tuesday night I excused myself a bit early because I was taking her to the hospital on the Wednesday morning. Those get-togethers with all the lads were great, and we had a few during the season. I know much has been made of Rangers' nights out in the past and it didn't seem to do them much harm. It didn't do us any harm either – apart from the occasional sore head!

I was at the hospital most of the Wednesday and was lucky enough to be there when my daughter Kira arrived. I've been at the births of both my children and it's a wonderful moment. Kira weighed in at a very healthy 9lbs 8 ozs and the doctors, including a Celtic fan, were great. I took champagne into the ground on the Thursday but Brian Scott said we should keep it for Saturday!

On the football front, we never gave Rangers' last game against Dundee United a thought during that last week and instead concentrated solely on ourselves. We knew our fate was still in our own hands and that was comforting. We knew we had a last chance to deliver.

So we took a vote and headed for Cameron House to

prepare. I roomed on my own, which I sometimes prefer, because I can get my head round it all when I'm there by myself. All sorts of thoughts were running through my head. We had to win. It was that simple. We had to take the title for ourselves and stop Rangers making it ten in a row. The former fact was straightforward enough, but I must admit I was also haunted by the prospect of being part of a Celtic team which had allowed Rangers to create a world record. That simply couldn't happen.

And it didn't. During the pre-match huddle Tom Boyd simply said 'This is it' and we emerged to a tumultuous reception. The noise was awesome. The stage was set.

Henrik Larsson gave us the perfect start with a wonderful goal that settled all the nerves, but although we had a few chances we had to wait for Harald to finish it off. As soon as he scored our second goal I knew that was it. We talked to each other and insisted we stayed calm, but it was difficult when you looked around. The noise was phenomenal. The fans knew their long wait was over and they were going for it big-time.

When the final whistle went, it was astonishing. I briefly thought that there we were, with a new coach and a new team, and we had done it. Mind you, I didn't have too much time to dwell on anything because Celtic Park was chaotic. I remembered Karl-Heinz Riedle phoning me after Liverpool played Celtic in the UEFA Cup and he was amazed at the sights he saw and the sounds he heard at the ground. I looked up and knew exactly what he meant. When Celtic fans raise their scarves and sing there's not many better sights and sounds in football. It is spectacular by any standards.

I was in among the lads, jumping about demented, and then I went to the side and threw my jersey into the crowd. Poor Saints were long gone, but they must have heard our dressing-room even on the road back to Perth. They certainly wouldn't have been caught in traffic, because no one inside the ground moved.

Champagne was flowing and it was bedlam. We put on 'Champions' T-shirts to collect the trophy, and then we put on others saying 'Smell the Glove', which caused some controversy and even now I don't pretend to understand it! I would have worn top hat and tails if they had asked, though. I was beyond caring. Snooker star John Higgins and comedian Billy Connolly were in amongst it all and I've never known scenes quite like it. The celebrations just seemed to go on and on.

It didn't take the lads long to get a bit drunk, because when you're on a high like that the champagne seems to take effect quicker! There were a few unusual sights. Craig Burley, for instance, didn't know what day it was. Mind you, I can't talk. I was into beer, champagne, cigars and even cigarettes. I think the only thing I didn't sample was dope!

In our defence, I would say we were all entitled to savour the moment. We had worked very hard for it and many's the time it's been said that the best team wins the league. That was us and it was a great feeling.

I eventually left Celtic Park about 8.30 p.m. – I think – but the good news was that I didn't have my car with me. I was picked up to go home because I had stuff with me to take on the club trip to Portugal the following day. Although the other lads were going out, I found Christopher and Kira crying when I got back so I didn't think it was very fair to leave Monica again, especially when I was going away the next morning.

Don't ask me why Celtic arranged the game against Sporting Lisbon for the midweek after the final league game of the season. I couldn't possibly answer that. It wasn't a good fixture to take on, or a good time to go. I know it had been arranged for a while but I still felt there should have been enough confidence shown in us to arrange for Celtic Park to be opened for the fans on the Sunday. There's no doubt in my mind we would have had another 50,000 in to see the league championship trophy and watch a lap of honour. We could have had another party.

Instead of that, a few sorry sights were winging their way to Portugal, where, it turned out, events were more like a wake than a celebration!

8

TRIUMPH TO DISASTER

I cannot believe that any club in the world other than Celtic would be able to turn a triumph into a disaster quite as quickly as we managed it after we won the Premier Division championship. It was incredible how we were celebrating one minute and virtually in mourning the next.

It's not easy to destroy something as good as a title win, especially when you've been waiting ten years for it, but Celtic managed it within a couple of days and that must be some kind of record. The whole Wim Jansen affair was bitterly disappointing from start to finish and even now I find it hard to understand how it was allowed to go quite as pear-shaped as it did.

I don't doubt there were faults on both sides but from a player's point of view I have to say I have nothing but respect for Wim and what he achieved in a very short space of time at Celtic Park. He took over at a difficult time, made some astute signings, won the Coca-Cola Cup and then, most important of all, guided the team to the league success that, as any Celtic fan will tell you, had been the Holy Grail for a decade. Others like Billy McNeill, Lou Macari, Liam Brady and Tommy Burns had failed to end Rangers' run but Jansen did and he deserves enormous credit for that.

I'm not privy to everything that happened behind the scenes, nor am I particularly interested, but I can say I was very disillusioned when he was allowed to leave the club. It just seems to me that a guy who achieved so much should have been encouraged to stay come hell or high water. It is inconceivable that he was able to walk away or, as has been widely indicated, leave before he was sacked. I know his departure left the squad absolutely shell-shocked. We had a fair inkling, along with everyone else, that all wasn't well but when it came to the crunch it was still a major blow.

The final decision came when we were on that ill-conceived trip to Portugal and the match against Sporting Lisbon which was part of the Jorge Cadete deal. We flew out there on a high, but it didn't take us long to crash back down to earth. When Wim told the players after dinner that he was leaving he didn't make a big deal of it – that wasn't his way about anything – but simply told us he was finishing. In these circumstances there's not much anyone can say although I think the players were shocked and disappointed at hearing the news, even though there had been rumblings beforehand.

Once the initial shock had disappeared I was left feeling disappointed and annoyed at the whole sorry saga. But I'm only a player and there was nothing then or now I could say or do to influence anything that went on. I maintain, however, that the affair was disastrous for the club and that the failure to appoint a successor for so long merely added to the whole unfortunate matter.

When Wim's departure became official, I don't think it helped, either, that he and the club became involved in a slanging match. That seemed a bit unnecessary on both sides, but clearly Wim felt he had to get a few things off his

ABOVE: The European Cup victory hits home. I pause to take it all in, as Andy Möller and Wolfgang Feiersinger share a joke

RIGHT: Karl-Heinz Riedle and I celebrate

Welcome to Celtic Park – the day I returned to Scotland from Germany

In action against Hearts, one of our close challengers in the 1997–98 season

ABOVE: Applause for the brilliant Celtic fans as I walk off with Craig Burley after another victory

RIGHT: I hardly broke sweat after going on as a substitute in the Coca-Cola Cup final, but I didn't mind sharing in the glory!

LEFT: One of the proudest moments of my career as I lift the Premier League Championship trophy aloft. Alan Stubbs is next to me, but don't ask what Tom Boyd is doing!

More action, against Andy Goram and Lorenzo Amoruso of Rangers

ABOVE AND RIGHT: Training with
Scotland: getting away from John
Collins and suffering with Eoin Jess

Tempers fray occasionally, and here Colin Hendry and I give Austria's Pieter Schotter a serious talking-to

Craig Brown and Alex Miller (out of the picture to the right) have just said something to make young lads Paul Gallacher and Kieran McAnespie, together with Craig Burley, Jackie McNamara, Tom Boyd and me, have a laugh

Now it's nearly the real thing as I look for the family in the Stade de France stand. Scott Booth and Jackie McNamara are doing likewise with the Scotland squad in the background

Look closely and you'll see I'm making a dent in the ball. Norway dented our World Cup hopes as well, and here are three of the culprits: Erik Rekdal, Staale Solbakken and Ronny Jonsson

TOP: My wife Monica and daughter Kira
BOTTOM LEFT: My son Christopher gets a close-up view of the European Cup
BOTTOM RIGHT: A winner: me with my Champions League winners' medal

chest – and, for that matter, the club obviously wanted its say as well. It all became a bit unsavoury, to say the least. When it was all going on – and being followed avidly on television and radio and in the newspapers – the players were trying to do their jobs. We lost narrowly in that match in Portugal in front of a handful of fans and, despite everything going on around us, we actually played quite well. That in itself was a minor miracle but if nothing else it showed the professionalism of the squad in trying circumstances.

By then the players were over the initial shock and it had been replaced by an inevitable feeling of uncertainty. Little discussions took place among the lads and the questions were always the same: who'll take over and will he want me? It made for a difficult summer, although my mind, and the minds of a lot of the squad, had to turn to the World Cup in France soon afterwards so we didn't get too much time to dwell on everything. But in the cold light of day, I remain bewildered that a club the size and stature of Celtic could allow events to take the form they did.

Anyway, in amongst that mayhem, no one could take the title away from us – or the Coca-Cola Cup, for that matter – and when you take Grant Mitchell of *Eastenders*, The Toothpick, Half-a-Brain and the Terrible Twins and get them coached by Willie Wonka, you can see it was no mean feat to win those two big prizes!

I had better explain. Those are a few of the nicknames of the lads who took Celtic to the biggest domestic success you can achieve. It's worth looking at them all in greater detail because whatever happens in the future they will be long remembered by a grateful support.

'Willie Wonka' is, of course, Wim. I first heard him called that by the lads on the way back from the Coca-Cola Cup final against Dundee United at Ibrox. The players were chanting: 'There's only one Willie Wonka, one Willie Wonka' – and it's fair to suggest it was something to do with his hair-do! I remember seeing Wim play – only on video, mind you! – and he's always had the same hairstyle. Did I really call it a style?

Anyway, hair apart, I have the utmost respect for Wim. I have worked with Scottish managers who like to shout and bawl but it's not coincidence that the three continental coaches I have had – Jansen, Ottmar Hitzfeld and Nevio Scala – don't go down that road. They have their say quietly and without fuss and from personal experience players tend to take more notice of that.

There were lots of things I could admire about Wim. His own playing record, for instance, was incredible and included two World Cup finals, which is something very few players can boast. That meant he had seen it and done it all, and that helped in his dealings with the Celtic lads. He would leave a decision on whether or not you wanted to play in the reserves on the way back from an injury to the player, for example, rather than telling you you had to play. I personally believe that experienced professionals don't need reserve-team football. If they train properly they'll be fit enough for the first team, and that seemed to be Wim's view as well.

He also developed a system and stuck to it. He wanted the ball played as quickly as possible and spread from side to side, and that worked well for us. Basically, he wanted good players to play and that's what we did. I thought he was first class and I had a lot of time for him.

His assistant Murdo MacLeod helped, of course, because we wouldn't have won things if they hadn't been working in harmony. They were a good partnership. The fact that Murdo knew Celtic inside out from his playing days obviously helped enormously, as did his local knowledge, because I don't think Wim would have known too much about Fir Park, Easter Road or East End Park before he came to Scotland! Murdo could fill in a few gaps and that was good.

However good the set-up is behind the scenes, though, it's the action on the park that counts and Celtic had good players. Let's start with Grant Mitchell or, if you prefer, Jonathan Gould. I must admit I didn't know too much about him when I came to Celtic but I do now. What a season he had, and if there was one save I remember in particular it has to be the one when he stopped a Derek Whyte effort at Aberdeen. Like so many of his saves, that one was vital because we ended up winning that match 1–0 through a Craig Burley penalty.

Mind you, we gave Jon some stick because he was a magnet for the media. He always seemed to be on the radio, on television or in the newspapers and I recall one day when he swore blind that that was it, he wasn't giving any more interviews. I told him there was no chance of that, but he insisted. So I went for a shower and afterwards walked out of the ground over to my car, switched on the radio and whose was the first voice I heard? You're right – the bold Jonathan was back inside the stadium, talking for Britain!

He has one other interesting side to him, and that is he never takes his car to training in case it gets dirty. It doesn't matter about anyone else's, though! Still, we put up with him because he's a smashing keeper and I was delighted to see him get to the World Cup in the summer. What a quantum leap from Bradford reserves to France '98!

Jackie McNamara was a very deserving winner of the Players' Player of the Year award and I was absolutely delighted for him. So much so, in fact, that he got me into a kilt for the first time when we all went to the awards ceremony decked out in the Celtic tartan. It will be the first of many major prizes for Jackie, I'm sure. He is a young lad who has everything going for him. Whenever he gets the ball you can hear the buzz of anticipation around the ground. He excites fans. He is quick and direct and they love that. I also think he'll get better now he has a bit of World Cup experience behind him and although he has had an unlucky injury the sky really is the limit. He and Simon Donnelly are the best of pals and apart from when they were separated at birth I think the only other person who has got between them is me – I change with that pair either side of me in the Celtic dressing-room.

In the middle of the defence you couldn't ask for anyone with more calm assurance than Marc Rieper. The big man is a commanding figure and not many players get the better of him either on the ground or in the air. That shouldn't be a surprise, I suppose, bearing in mind how often he has played for Denmark, but in amongst all those caps I can't imagine he has ever played better than he did in our title-winning season. He and Alan Stubbs seemed made for each other and were formidable.

Marc isn't flamboyant in any way but simply gets on with his job and every team needs someone like him. Alan is a far better player than some people give him credit for and I have to say I was surprised last year when he didn't make it into any of the England get-togethers. I watched them play a 'B' match at one point ahead of the World Cup and I remember thinking that Stubbsy was certainly as good as, if not better than, anything on show. He really doesn't make many mistakes at all. He's calm and assured on the ball and is good with both feet. He also hits a terrific long pass when he can pick out anyone and he's a real threat to the opposition when he joins the attack. I would be surprised if he hadn't been in the running for the 1997–98 season's Player of the Year award. He likes a laugh, which is great, but when he lapses into that Liverpool accent of his he loses me.

The only name you could have for Tom Boyd would be Mr Celtic. He's our captain and a terrific one into the bargain. Off the pitch he organises things like nights out for the lads and makes sure everything is okay. On the park he is excellent. He's quick and decisive, and after suffering so much as a Celtic player over recent years, I don't think anyone could have been happier at our successes last term. Being captain of the Celtic championship-winning team was something and I think, apart from anything else, it was a huge weight off his shoulders.

Stephane Mahe is one of those foreigners who doesn't speak a lot of English but somehow understands everything you say to him. I think he kids us on about how much of our language he talks. You certainly understand him just fine on the park, where he had an excellent season on the left-hand side of the defence. Stephane is a strong lad who spends some time in the gym and I don't think he loses too many 50-50 tackles. We missed him a bit when he wasn't playing because he gave us good balance.

I felt really sorry for Craig Burley when he was sent off playing for Scotland against Morocco in the World Cup because it was an unfortunate end to a fantastic season. He'll get over it, of course, because he's that kind of character but it was disappointing, especially so after his brilliant goal against Norway in the previous match.

There's no doubt that Craig much prefers the midfield role he operates so well for Celtic, and it was an eye-opener to me during the 1997-98 season because previously I had only seen him playing for Scotland in the right wing-back position he's not keen on. But I can see why he prefers his Celtic role because he had a great year and scored some wonderful – and crucial – goals for the club. I felt we struck up a good understanding in midfield and it suits him because he gets all the glory while I'm covering his back! Seriously, though, he deserved to win the Scottish Football Writers' Player of the Year award.

I shared a room at France '98 with CB and if I have an abiding memory of that it's those famous teeth grinning up at me from a dish next to the washhand basin every time I went into the bathroom! Craig likes a laugh, too, and I remember giving him some stick at our Barrowfield training ground one day when the place was a mudbath yet his boots were spotless at the end of the session. It's the only time I've been able to argue with his contribution.

Generally, Craig gets the credit he deserves, but you can't say the same for Morten Wieghorst who, for me, is a very underrated player. I must admit even I didn't realise how good he was until I played alongside him. Mort likes to play the game the proper way and there aren't many players in Scotland with more skill. He is technically very gifted and does more for the side than I suspect some people might imagine. I was pleased when I heard in the summer that after long negotiations he had decided to stay at Celtic. He would have been a hard player to replace, although he's been unlucky with injury this term.

Another player who has been vitally important to us has been Henrik Larsson. He's a bit like Brian Laudrup was to Rangers or Andy Möller was to Borussia Dortmund simply because he can make things happen out of nothing, and that is a special bonus to any team. He has a good pedigree, of course, with Feyenoord and Sweden and it's easy to see why. He works hard in training but really turns it on when it matters. He has a lovely touch, links the play well and scores goals, which isn't a bad combination.

Henrik also forged a good relationship with Harald Brattbakk when the Norwegian arrived at Celtic Park. It maybe took Harald a little bit of time to settle but that's normal and I felt he took an enormous amount of unfair criticism. Anyone with his track record at Rosenborg had to be a good player, and I was absolutely delighted when he showed that and proved a few people wrong with his goals. I don't like seeing fellow professionals get a hard time. He was turned over by one or two newspapers near the end of the season, but it's a measure of his popularity that we all decided there and then to stop giving interviews. He was very hard done by, even though he doesn't have a bad bone in his body. Which brings me nicely to his nickname of The Toothpick. He's so thin he clearly needs a good helping of mince and tatties! Yet a classic example of how good he is was his goal in that critical last game of the season against St Johnstone. The pace he showed was phenomenal and I was really pleased he scored the goal.

Those lads were the nucleus of the team but you don't win anything nowadays – as France proved during the

World Cup – with just 11 players. Football is more and more a squad game, and with the ever-increasing risks of suspensions allied to the inevitable injuries, I believe that a first-team pool of a minimum of 20 is required by the top clubs. We escaped relatively lightly in the 1997–98 season in terms of both injury and suspension but we still needed every available body to see us through the winter – and that meant that a whole load of other guys were absolutely vital to the team and the winning of the title.

Take Darren Jackson, for instance. 'Half-a-Brain' was incredible. To come back from the kind of major operation he had – hence the nickname – to play a part for Celtic and then go to the World Cup was a magnificent feat. It spoke volumes for his courage and ability and I was pleased he was at France '98. Darren is a smashing lad and a good player. He has a terrific engine and more skill than some might think. He is also very funny when he's not going about his business. He winds me up all the time and I have to laugh. He looks at my Rolex watch and my nice car, for example, and tells me when I was at Motherwell it was a Swatch and a Fiesta! I have to say, though, that I have never known anyone who likes the sun as much. He's always on the sunbed in Glasgow and when we were at the World Cup he was sun-worshipper full time and Scotland star part time!

I've mentioned Enrico Annoni elsewhere in this book because of the job he did marking Brian Laudrup during the 1997–98 season, and I can't imagine there's a better man-marker in the country, which probably owes every-thing to his Serie A background. He's a tremendously strong lad who is built like a brick outhouse and that means not too many beat him in a tackle. He enjoys all the dressing-room crack as well, even though he gets pelters about wearing odd-coloured boots and, occasionally, a bandana.

I would like to see Regi Blinker do well because, despite some fans' misgivings, he can play. He took a bit of stick during the double-winning season and I think that got to him, but he can come through that and prove the doubters wrong. Generally he's a chirpy lad to have about the place and I like him. He's due a wee break, which hopefully will happen now.

Tosh McKinlay was unlucky last year. Wim Jansen clearly preferred Stephane to Tosh, and that was simply down to personal preference. I don't actually think there's much between the two players, but Wim made his choice. Tosh certainly has a left foot that is as sweet as a nut. He can put the ball anywhere with it, although I would admit the same can't be said for his other one!

I've known Tosh for a long time now; in fact, we went to Bayer Leverkusen together for trials more years ago than I care to remember. Unfortunately, his patter hasn't changed in the intervening years. When the lads had a night out during the '97–'98 season we all went looking like tramps – yet there was Tosh looking like a pimp or Huggy Bear in his trendy suit. He has the cheek, too, to give me stick about my shoes, which I buy in Germany and which, I can assure you, are quite pricey. Still, Regi Blinker likes them because he's asked me to get him some next time I'm over.

Simon Donnelly is the other half of the Terrible Twins with Jackie McNamara. He's a smashing player and the pair have carried their friendship on to the park a lot, which is great because they're obviously on the same wavelength. Sid is technically sound and one of the most elusive players I've seen, because when he knocks it past you it's a struggle to get to him. There's no doubt in my mind that his best years are ahead of him and I hope for Celtic's sake that both he and his big pal stay at the club for a long time. So do hordes of screaming girls!

You couldn't get an unluckier player than Tommy Johnson, who has had more than his fair share of injuries since he came to Celtic Park. Yet throughout all the hard times he's remained chirpy, at least publicly, and he loves a laugh. I do hope he gets a decent break and if he does it will be like Celtic signing a new player – and a good one at that.

I knew Phil O'Donnell at Fir Park and I have always liked him. He too has been very unlucky with injuries but when he's fit he's a marvellous player who is a bit different, and that makes him very useful. Phil can get in behind defences almost without them noticing and I think Celtic – and, for that matter, Scotland – could use a player like that. He's another I would love to see get a really good run without any problems.

You couldn't meet a nicer guy than David Hannah, or a better professional. David found himself either on the substitutes bench or out of the squad altogether at times during the 1997–98 season yet he never moaned. He got on with his training, worked hard in the gym and was always ready when he received the call. There was never a huff; he just did the job that was required of him and did it well. The benefit for a coach in having someone like David is that he can play in so many positions, although I'm not sure that versatility has helped him.

Malky Mackay, now of Norwich City, is another who didn't appear to hold grudges when he wasn't in the team – and, believe me, that is not the case with every player. Yet the big man came in and performed well when needed and he's a good professional. Good luck to him.

I felt sorry for Stewart Kerr, who was injured first of all and then found Jonathan Gould blocking his path to a first-team place. But he is still young and it wouldn't surprise me in the least if he was a Scotland goalkeeper in years to come. It's certainly all there for him.

Wee Brian McLaughlin, like some of the other lads, struggled with injury at different times but I like his style. It is very difficult getting the ball off him. He's very skilful and a tricky player to play against.

Then there's Paul Lambert. I must confess that while a few of the lads have their own wee superstitions, I think I have enough for the rest of the squad put together. It's strange, really, because I was never superstitious until I went to Germany. I've made up for it since, though.

I was given the number 14 jersey at Borussia Dortmund, for instance, and that is my favourite number. I selected it when I was at the World Cup with Scotland and if I'm ever given the choice that's the one I'll go for. Strangely, when I moved back to Scotland I discovered my new house was number 14. Scary or what!

Then there's the pig. I had better explain. When I was at Dortmund an old lady came to training and gave me what she called a good-luck pig. She was a lovely soul and often invited Monica round for coffee. She insisted this pig would bring me good luck so, naturally, I took it every-where with me and still have it.

As I've already mentioned, I always eat the same meal the night before a game and on match day, and I also go to bed at midnight the night before a match. I always wear a T-shirt under my jersey when I'm playing as well. And I carry a photograph of my children, Kira and Christopher, wherever I go.

Actually, there are so many superstitions that it has become a complete nightmare trying to remember them all to go through the same rituals! But, generally speaking, they have brought me a lot of luck in the last couple of years and I'm not about to ditch them.

There's one other person I really should mention in amongst all this and that's Brian Scott, who is unquestion-ably the best physio I've ever worked with. But he's also more than that. You can go to Brian with any problem and he'll do his best to help. He's a guy you can rely on totally. He also likes a laugh, and he gives me abuse about the tape I use for my socks and moans that he can only get it in Germany, when all the time I know he has a store of it in the cupboard in his room.

In that most crucial of all seasons last year we had a strange but successful mix of characters around Celtic Park. Each and every one of them contributed to the club's success.

Now, if everything is equal, I would like to stay at Celtic Football Club for the rest of my career. I put in the initial qualification simply because, as I've often said before, I refuse to take anything for granted in football. You simply don't know what's around the corner in this game. However, there's no doubt that if we continue to progress I would like to be part of it all until I hang up my boots. I don't want to leave.

You don't always get what you want in football or in life, of course, and as with any job there is a down side. But more of that later. All I can say is that it was a fantastic move for me to come to Celtic when I came back to Scotland from Germany, and even in the year or so I was away this club had grown at an incredible rate. Now, when you look around, you see a magnificent stadium that would grace any club in any country in the world, a ground that is packed week in, week out by supporters who are second to none, and a great bunch of lads, as I have already described.

Celtic Park itself is the envy of so many clubs. More than one visiting player has said to me, especially this season, how spectacular it is now that the new Jock Stein Stand has completed the picture and who am I to argue? From my point of view it is a privilege and a pleasure to be able to play there regularly. That is especially the case when you consider the fans. I can't think of any other club that would attract 60,000 people, as a matter of course, to friendly, pre-season or testimonial matches. I also can't imagine there are many other supporters who would have stuck with their team quite the way the Celtic fans did when Rangers were winning just about everything in sight for the best part of a decade. It must have hurt like hell, yet they continued to back the side and have at last reaped some kind of reward.

They were entitled to enjoy themselves when we won the Premier League and Coca-Cola Cup double in the 1997–98 season, and the championship, naturally, was *the* prize. They suffered as Rangers became joint world-record holders with nine titles in a row, and ten would surely have been too much to bear. This club owed them, and I was delighted to be part of the side that finally delivered. It just meant so much, it's difficult for outsiders to understand. If they had been where I was on 9 May, though, they would have understood. One look from the pitch into the stands and the thousands of faces there and they would have realised that all the pain and suffering, if not exactly worth it, was finally almost bearable. It was a magic moment. As for the players, I've already given them enough credit and I would hate to let any heads get swollen!

So, basically, I'm happy. And I'll continue to be as long as Jozef Venglos or whoever is coach here is happy with me, believes in my ability and wants me to be part of the set-up at Celtic Park. Even the rumour factory that has churned out stories about various clubs being interested in me in recent months doesn't bother me. I've heard Leeds United mentioned regularly, there was talk briefly of Juventus and it has also been suggested that I will team up again with Ottmar Hitzfeld at Bayern Munich. It's flattering but a bit unfair to be linked with other clubs and I know, for instance, that I would find it very difficult to go to Munich if that fiction ever became fact. I don't honestly think I could ever play for a club in Germany other than Dortmund. I was treated so well there by the club and the fans that I would feel a traitor if I went elsewhere.

It is not an issue, anyway, although when I say I am happy as long as the Celtic coach wants me, I have to recognise that others at Celtic Park may not. It has been fairly well documented that general manager Jock Brown doesn't appear to rate me and, as I've already explained, at first that gave me a problem. I had heard the same story from several reputable sources and to say I was a bit upset around the time of my transfer is putting it mildly. Now, though, I've mellowed a bit insofar as I have decided that if that is his opinion of me, so be it. I have opinions as well and everyone is entitled to his or hers. You don't even have to like them particularly. And that's just one of his I don't.

What I don't have to do, either, is have anything more to do with the general manager than is absolutely necessary. Obviously I will go to supporters' functions or whatever, but otherwise I don't need any real involvement with Jock Brown – and perhaps that is just as well because we are clearly opposites that don't attract.

Aside from knowing very early on in my Celtic career that he hadn't been keen to get me and that it was only because Wim Jansen and Murdo MacLeod kept pushing for me that I finally arrived, I have had other differences of opinion with him. One memorable one concerned what he called 'media training'. Basically, it seemed he wanted me to learn how to deal with the press. Maybe he should have suggested a course in how to deal with general managers instead, because the plan got short shrift. It's not my job to learn his version – or anyone else's – of how I should talk to people. In the main, I have always got along fine with the media anyway, although I confess I don't particularly seek them out. But I have dealt with them often enough in Scotland, in Germany, in France at the World Cup and in various other countries when it's been required. I have no problem with continuing to deal with them as and when it's required. What I do have a problem with, though, is being told how to do it. The idea never got off the ground and we had what is called a full and frank exchange of views about the matter. Maybe some guys would have been happy to go along with it – some at the club possibly even did – but it wasn't for me. I am at Celtic to play football to the best of my ability and my only aim is to make the club successful. That's it. Period.

I have two and a half years left on my contract, which will take me up to very nearly 32 years of age, and maybe I will still be good enough by then to earn a new deal so I can end my playing days at Celtic Park. If that doesn't work out then hopefully I'll still be good enough to play at a high level with another club because many people – including Wim Jansen, whose judgement I respect – have told me to play as long as I can. One other person I like and admire hugely has also given me sound advice about playing on as I get older and although few, if any, people in this country will know him, the football fans should certainly recognise the name of Toni Schumacher.

Toni had a wonderful playing career and was one of the great German goalkeepers, yet he will forever be best remembered for an unfortunate incident during the 1982 World Cup when he was involved in a terrible collision with Patrick Battiston of France who, unfortunately, suffered a bad injury. The referee took no action at the time but afterwards, when people reviewed the challenge time and again on television, Toni was pilloried for it and the moment remains to many people his main claim to fame.

I have to admit that when I got to know him – he was goalkeeping coach at Dortmund – I found it impossible to believe he had deliberately hurt Battiston. You couldn't meet a nicer man. I remember asking him about the incident and he was happy enough to talk about it. He stressed that it had been in no way intentional and that as he'd come out to meet the ball he had turned slightly and that was how Battiston had been so badly hurt.

It's sad that he is recalled for that incident in many places, because in others he is remembered for working with kids. When we played Galatasaray in the Champions League the Turkish fans applauded him because he had worked for a youngsters' charity when he had played at Fenerbahce. That is more the Toni I know. He is such an enthusiast and will go out of his way to help you. He's now manager of Fortuna Cologne, so I hope everything works out for him there. I'll probably find out in due course because he wants to come over here and play golf at some point and we keep in fairly regular contact with each other.

When people like Toni and Wim tell me to play on, I admit I want to do that – although there is a qualification. I don't want to drop down the leagues and trawl my way through the lower divisions. At least that's the way I feel now. Maybe when it gets nearer the time I'll be grateful to do even that, but somehow I doubt it.

What I might do is drop further back in the team. Other midfield men have become defenders – Matthias Sammer and Lothar Matthaus are two classic examples – and that is always a possibility when the legs go a little. I actually played at the back for Dortmund once, against Hansa Rostock, and quite enjoyed the experience so maybe there's a whole new career there for me. I'll certainly know when it's time to call it a day totally, though, and I won't wait to be told by others. Hopefully that will be as a Celtic player.

After that, who knows? I would like to stay in the game as a coach first and then as a manger or, rather, head coach. I know I'll need to go through the appropriate coaching courses because you need a licence to operate in many countries nowadays but I'm happy enough to do that.

One thing that intrigued me recently as well was the idea mooted by former England star David Platt. It seems he had been offered numerous player-coach jobs when he was still at Arsenal, but instead of jumping in he decided to retire from playing and has said he is going to take a year out, travel to different clubs around the world and learn as much as he can from a variety of coaches. That seems a pretty sensible idea and one I would certainly consider.

I have, in fact, already made a bit of a start towards becoming a coach because when I was in Germany I kept a kind of diary of just about everything we did at Borussia Dortmund in terms of training methods, diets and general facts and figures that might come in useful some day. A bit of sensible forward planning!

I also listened long and hard to coaches like Hitzfeld and Scala and hopefully will have picked up something from spending time with them. It would have been criminal not to. They are acknowledged experts and if you can't learn at the feet of the masters, who can you learn from? Whatever happens, and if I'm lucky enough to become a coach, I'll be as near a European one as I can be. They are the best.

That's the Lambert masterplan right now, but if a week is a long time in politics, a few years is an absolute lifetime in football. Right now, thinking about today is really enough to keep me fully occupied. I don't need to look too far ahead. What will be, will be.

9

COACHES AND
THE PERFECT TEN

I have now played under a dozen managers or coaches –
whichever term you prefer – and while that might seem
quite a lot to some people, I'm not taking the rap for them
getting sacked or leaving the clubs I've been at. It's just
coincidence, honestly!

Some have been outstanding, some have been good and
some, well, some I haven't seen eye to eye with. But that's
football. It would be a poorer sport if all coaches were
clones of one other. What I would say, however, is that of
them all, the guys I have admired the most have been
foreigners. They approach the game differently from our
coaches and as far as I'm concerned the continental way is
the way to go.

Foreign managers or coaches are a fairly recent innova-
tion in Britain with the odd exception over the years.
Celtic's own Dr Jozef Venglos had a previous life at Aston

Villa but was considered by chairman Doug Ellis to be ahead of his time for this country. Well, his time and that of other foreigners has certainly arrived now and I would be surprised if more and more clubs don't go down that road in future.

You only have to look at the 1997–98 season to get some idea of how successful they can be. Those who said at the start of the season that coaches like Wim Jansen or Arsène Wenger would struggle to adapt to our game must have choked on their words. Wim, of course, won the Coca-Cola Cup and Premier League with Celtic and Wenger took Arsenal to the English double of Premiership and FA Cup. Not bad for two guys who certainly attracted their fair share of doubters before they started. The people who didn't give them a chance wore blinkers – and not Regi's! We have a tendency to be a bit insular in Britain when it comes to looking towards the continent but maybe we've learned the lesson now. To be fair, I was the same before I went to Germany but I certainly lost my 'island mentality' during my spell in Dortmund.

The successes of Jansen and Wenger obviously stirred other clubs into action and it was interesting during last summer to see men like Dick Advocaat follow Walter Smith into the Rangers job and Gerard Houllier join Roy Evans at Liverpool. Two big clubs going continental – although I must confess I hope one of them isn't too successful!

So my preference will always be for a foreign coach, although that's not to say I haven't learned something from all the managers I've played under. Everyone has something to offer – it's just that some have more than others, as far as I'm concerned.

I have to go back some time to my first manager in professional football. He was Ricky MacFarlane at St Mirren. It was he who signed me on an 'S' form for the Love Street club so if you have a problem about me then he's the one to blame! I'm grateful to Ricky because he gave me that start but I never got to know him very well because he resigned from the Saints job, in controversial circum-stances, not long after he signed me. He always seemed a nice guy, though, and even now I bump into him occasion-ally and we have a chat about those days and Saints in general. But I could never say I really knew how good, bad or indifferent he was as a manager, which makes an opinion difficult.

Next up was Alex Miller and I honestly don't have a bad word to say about him. I've mentioned elsewhere how important it was for me to have someone like Alex in charge of St Mirren when I was just starting out. It could all have gone horribly wrong without too much effort, but Alex ensured I picked up the right habits. He was pretty hot on discipline, but I can certainly see the benefit of that now. I like to think I learned a lot more about what's right than what's wrong in the game from Alex, who in turn must have learned all he knew from his spell as a player at Rangers. I certainly had him as a manager at just the right point of my career.

He was followed into the Love Street hot-seat by Alex Smith and he, too, was very influential in my career. First of all he is a very nice man, which is a start in any job, although, to be fair, maybe not always in football. But, more importantly, from the game's point of view he was tremendous with young players and knew exactly how to bring them on. The youngsters at Love Street at the time all learned an enormous amount from Alex and I would imagine there are players around the country who are just as grateful to him as I am. I think what was important too was that we could see he had the respect of the senior players at the time. If a manager has older, more experi-enced players on his side it is a huge bonus and something younger lads don't miss.

St Mirren being St Mirren, however, Alex was treated scandalously. He won the Scottish Cup for the club and no one should ever underestimate that achievement. That kind of success comes along once in a blue moon for a club the size of Saints and Alex should really have been given the freedom of Paisley. Instead, not long afterwards he was sacked and it was a shocking way for him to be treated after what he did for St Mirren. I might add he suffered the same fate at Aberdeen and from all I know of that it was an equally sad and shabby way to deal with a fine manager.

I would have no hesitation in saying that Alex, outside of the foreigners, is the best man-manager I have worked with. He seemed to know how to treat players, young or old, experienced or inexperienced. It was good being at Saints at the same time as him.

All of which made it even more difficult for me to work well with the next man into the Paisley club, Tony Fitzpatrick. Let me say immediately that Tony has black-and-white blood in his veins, because he played for the club and has managed them twice. He is a St Mirren man through and through. That is fair enough. But I have to say we didn't always see eye to eye. In fact, we rarely saw eye to eye. It was an uneasy relationship for much of the time we were together as player and manager at Love Street and especially so in the later stages.

Tony, to be fair, had his way of doing things and he clearly believed in them. I have no problem with that. Every manager is the same. It's just that you can go along with some, whilst others rub you the wrong way. I found that Tony never had any room for compromise. It was his way or no way at all and especially since I have worked with foreign coaches I have found that to be a mistake. Even then, when I was relatively young, I found it difficult to handle and we had our fair share of ups and downs and differences of opinion. The final insult was the price tag he put on me. I was still a relatively untried youngster, yet St Mirren wanted a big transfer fee. I think it was just his way of hurting me and that was disappointing.

So I didn't shed many tears when Tony left and was replaced by Davie Hay and I didn't have any problems with him. Davie managed like he played – hard but fair. He let you know exactly where you stood and I appreciated that. Davie, though, was only at Love Street for a year or so, and because of that I can't really say he was a huge influence on my career one way or another. But I liked him anyway.

Saints at that time seemed to have a revolving door when it came to managers coming and going. The Love Street hot-seat is more like an electric chair. It has always struck me as a shame that they regularly threaten to be a big club but never quite make it. Sure, there are occasions – like that Scottish Cup win – when they are right up there with the best of them, but it's never often enough or consistently enough, and maybe the turnover of managers has something to do with that. I'm not suggesting they could ever rival Celtic or Rangers, who have the kind of fan-pulling power Saints can only dream of, but I see no reason why at some point they couldn't be a Dundee United or a Kilmarnock. Love Street is fine, the fans are out there and it just needs something to get the place going. That something is money, most probably, and that is always a problem but maybe backing the right man and giving him a bit of time would help.

Anyway, Jimmy Bone was next in line and I enjoyed my time at Love Street with him in charge. He was another who liked the young players at the club to learn the right habits and at that point there were some pretty good youngsters on the books who were well looked after. JB was always fair as well, and that's important. He was a great character into the bargain and a tremendous motivator, and whether it was training or a game he did his best to make it enjoyable for the players.

I left Love Street when Jimmy was boss but it wouldn't have mattered who was in charge, because the parting of the ways was inevitable by then. I think he was sorry to see me go but, equally, I'm sure he understood my reasons. I had reached the stage where I needed a new platform or my career was going to stand still.

The man who gave me that fresh start has taken some stick over the years yet if I haven't done it before I would like to thank Tommy McLean here and now for saving my career. Believe me, that's not too melodramatic. He may not be everyone's cup of tea but he'll do for me. He gave me a chance to continue and better myself in football when others wouldn't and for that I will be eternally grateful.

I've heard over the years all the horror stories about Tam and, indeed, the rest of the McLean clan but you can only take people as you find them and I never had a real problem with him when we were both at Motherwell. Sure, he can be hard on you – some would say unfair – but I always believed he was doing it for your benefit, not his, and you can't argue with that. He was – is – a vastly experienced manager who knew his way about after a terrific playing career and I was quite happy to listen to any advice he gave me. I would have been foolish not to.

I have to say, too, that the majority of the advice he gave me was sound. He knew what he was talking about and I had a lot of time for him. He was a big help to me, firstly by taking me to Fir Park and then by encouraging me while I was there. I enjoyed some good times at 'Well under wee Tam and I was sorry to see him go.

Unfortunately, those good times didn't continue under his successor Alex McLeish. Well, actually, they did initially because in Eck's first season, when he was using Tommy's players, we finished second in the league and that doesn't often happen to Motherwell! It was a really good year and I felt Alex handled everything pretty well. He obviously recognised that the squad he had inherited had some decent players and by and large he didn't change that much. I don't know what happened after that to make him change his mind, but things between him and me went from good to bad to worse. A decent working relationship made way for arguments and it all went sour for me at Fir Park over a period of time. It wasn't much fun to be spending half my career arguing with the manager.

So it all went a bit pear-shaped and hardly a week went by without Alex and me having a shouting match about something. We just couldn't agree on anything and it made for some difficult times there. I'm sure we both said things in the heat of the moment we have regretted since and certainly we speak now whenever we see each other. There are absolutely no problems. But at the time Alex simply didn't believe I would go abroad, and even if I did I knew he thought I wouldn't make it and that I would be on the next plane back home, probably begging to be taken back on again at Fir Park. Maybe from that point of view I should be grateful to him because his lack of belief certainly spurred me on.

I genuinely don't know if Alex simply didn't rate me or whether he would have maybe liked to have spent some time abroad himself, because he played his entire career at Aberdeen and didn't take the opportunities to go to the continent that I'm sure must have been presented to a player of his calibre at club and country level. Whatever the reason or reasons, I don't think either of us was too sorry to see the back of the other when I went abroad and I did make a decent go of it in Germany with Borussia Dortmund.

And it was there I came across probably the best coach I have worked with through all the years at all my clubs. Ottmar Hitzfeld, together with his assistant Michael Henke, made my career what it is today. Of that there can be no doubt. Others, like Ricky MacFarlane and Alex Miller, started it off the right way. Alex Smith continued it, as did Tommy McLean, but Hitzfeld made it. He was the main man as far as I'm concerned. If I have achieved anything in football – and I like to think I have – then it's been largely down to him and I owe him the biggest thanks of all. It would be silly to speculate on what might have happened to me if Ottmar hadn't taken me on at Dortmund, but it is right and proper to acknowledge his influence. It was huge. From the moment he transformed me from an offensive midfield player who had been played almost as a winger in Scotland to a more defensive and central role, through to the moment I left Germany for Celtic, he was my mentor.

So just what made him so special? First of all his man-management was absolutely spot on. He took care of players, he listened to them and because of that he got the best out of them. I was the new kid on the block so maybe I was easy to impress, but remember that Ottmar was also dealing with more experienced, big-name stars like Andy Möller, Jurgen Kohler and Matthias Sammer, and there were other nationalities involved as well, like Paulo Sousa and Julio Cesar. It was a fairly cosmopolitan mix of some of the best players in Europe yet he handled them all superbly without ever appearing, to me at least, to have favourites. Everyone appeared to be treated in the same way, and when you think of the company I was keeping, that was a big thing.

He was also very tactically astute. He would see things very quickly and make the necessary changes, and while he was doing his thing the knock-on effect was that it made me far more tactically aware as well. Ottmar also never lost the plot – at least not in front of the players. He wasn't one for ranting and raging and throwing managerial tantrums – or, for that matter, throwing teacups across the dressing-room! Instead he made his points quietly yet forcibly and, more often than not, to you personally. He wasn't into doing what some managers do, making a fool of a player while everyone else looks on. He would rather get the player aside in a quiet moment and speak to him then. It seemed to me to be a sensible way of going about it. And no one can argue that his way was anything other than hugely success-ful. He must have been doing something right to have won the Bundesliga twice and then the European Cup.

He and Michael are now at Bayern Munich and I hope they get a lot of success there as well. But whatever they do, their achievements at Dortmund will always be remembered and appreciated by the fans there. Likewise with me. I owe them a huge debt of gratitude.

The pair must have been a hard act to follow for Nevio Scala. After all, you can't do much more at club level in Europe than win the Champions League. It meant that he took on an awesome task and, indeed, he was only at Dortmund for a year. It was a very difficult time for the club, even allowing for previous successes. I left and so did Karl-Heinz Riedle and Paulo Sousa. On top of that, Matthias Sammer was injured much of the time. It was a really transitional season for Borussia and therefore a very hard time for a new coach to make any kind of impression. I was there for only the first part of his spell but I have to say I was very, very impressed with Scala. He seemed a genuinely nice man and he was certainly good for me in the brief time we worked together. He liked football to be played the way it should be played, which must count for something.

I found in my time in Germany that you have to work with foreign coaches to know just how good they are. I could go on and on about them and the many and varied qualities the top guys have, but you really have to experience it first hand. I was lucky enough to do that and they certainly struck a chord with me. That's why I was delighted when I knew it was Wim Jansen – even if it was only him – who wanted me at Celtic. I didn't know him personally but I knew about his background as a great player for Holland and I knew a bit about his managerial exploits.

Even so, I wouldn't have judged him until I had worked with him. As it happens, I took to Wim immediately. One reason may well have been that he at least seemed to have been desperate to get me into his team and that obviously sits well with any player. But there was much more to my admiration for the Dutchman than simply that. He had the same man-management gift that the continentals generally seem to have insofar as he was always available to talk to. I have gone on about him elsewhere in this book as well, but it's worth repeating that the success he achieved at Celtic had eluded a lot of other managers over the years. I thoroughly enjoyed my time working with Wim and, as I have pointed out, I was very sorry to see him go.

It was disappointing when he left, but I knew I could still phone him if I needed advice and I appreciated that. As a man he is terrific and as a coach I put him right up there with the best of them, which for me means Hitzfeld and Scala. I am sure he will achieve lots more success and that will simply underline how remarkable his achievements in Scotland were. He left a huge gap at Celtic Park and the events of the summer proved how hard he was to replace, whatever anyone might say.

Eventually the club appointed Dr Jozef Venglos to succeed Wim and Eric Black became his number two. As I write it's really · too early for me to pass a thoroughly considered judgement on the partnership from my point of view. To follow Wim Jansen was always going to be difficult. It could have been Mario Zagallo or Aime Jacquet and it would have been hard. Whoever came in was going to need time – and, of course, that is hardly in plentiful supply when you are a manager or a coach.

In the early days of Dr Jo's reign, though, I would have to say I found him similar in many ways to Wim. He is a nice man and very approachable. He understands the need to have a two-way conversation and, indeed, seems to enjoy that. Like Wim and other foreigners he also seems to be 100 per cent behind the players and their needs, and that is appreciated by the guys in the dressing-room.

Eric, according to some people, is being groomed to eventually succeed Venglos as coach of the club but I wouldn't know about that. He took over on a temporary basis when we were waiting for an appointment and he is pretty heavily involved as assistant now.

I always like to give a coach time before I form an opinion and ideally I would like to see what happens to Celtic this season. I will say, however, that players and fans alike expect to see the progress started by Wim continuing.

Everyone wants more success, more trophies and more days like those when we won the Coca-Cola Cup and the Premier League championship in the 1997–98 season. That's the nature of the beast. Time, therefore, will tell.

The number ten was a constant theme that season as we tried to stop Rangers setting a world record and for many it might be immediately associated with a well-known residence in London's Downing Street, but for me it means the jersey worn by some of the greatest players in the world. I have always looked, for no particular reason, at stars with a number ten on their back and thought they were special, although it was really Ottmar Hitzfeld who brought it home to me when he pointed out that many are the playmakers of their teams, the guys who make sides tick and who make it all happen. And when I look at my time in the game – and even before that – the case is proved beyond any reasonable doubt. These guys have a special kind of magic.

Look at Pele, for a start. I have only ever seen him on television but there's no doubt he was the greatest player ever. He had so much skill it was scary, and it was probably him who made the number ten jersey what it is. The games I have seen of him playing in the 1970 World Cup were amazing. He seemed to be able to do things no one else could do then and no one else has been able to do since. I would have loved to have seen him play myself.

Then there was Maradona. He was playing when I was growing up and I can remember thinking that no player could possibly ever match his skill. His 'Hand of God' goal for Argentina against England might not have been the best illustration of his talent but the one that followed in that famous World Cup tie certainly was. He picked the ball up inside his own half and then promptly took on and beat about six English players before planting the ball past Peter Shilton. It was sensational and has to be one of the greatest goals ever scored. The tragedy of Maradona, of course, is that his career hit the skids through allegations of drug abuse and it seemed that no matter how hard he tried to get back he never quite made it.

It's astonishing when you look through football history just how many of the genuinely talented players have self-destructed. Maybe it is that incredible ability – and the hype that goes with it – that puts these guys over the edge but I think it is a terrible waste.

Still, Pele and Maradona remain among the best players the world has ever seen, although there have been plenty of other big names who have worn that number ten jersey. I have encountered a few of them at closer quarters.

Andy Möller is certainly one of them. He is undoubtedly one of the most gifted players I have ever played alongside and not many could touch him when he was on his game. He had everything going for him. He had pace and ability. Some players have pace and are clumsy, but Andy was well balanced. He had an amazing gift as well for being able to produce the unexpected, and that helped him win games for both Borussia and Germany more times than I care to remember. The Bundesliga was awash with quality for a long time but there haven't been too many better than Andy.

One guy I wished I had had as a team-mate when I was in Germany was Thomas Hassler, who, unfortunately, then played for Karlsruhe and gave me a very hard time whenever we met on the field. Hassler, ironically now at Dortmund, was smaller than Möller and, indeed, played a little bit deeper but he really was a first-class player. He could turn a game with just one flash of magic.

There were a few other players in Germany when I was there who graced the number ten jersey apart from these two. Another, unquestionably, was Krasimir Balakov of Stuttgart who, like Hassler, was small but deadly. The Bulgarian certainly knew how to damage teams. He hit them where it hurt and was a very difficult opponent to tie down.

And then, of course, there was Lothar Matthaus. I played

against him and Bayern Munich quite early in my Dortmund career and I always remember him wishing me good luck in Germany, which was a nice gesture. I also swapped shirts with him after that match – something that's done regularly at Bundesliga games – and I'll cherish that.

Matthaus has been a marvellous player at club and country level and he has shown his quality by moving from midfield to defence, where he looks just as comfortable as ever. What he may have lost in pace he makes up for with experience and anyone arriving from the moon would surely think he had occupied a defensive role all his life. He is one of the genuinely great players.

I came up against Zinedine Zidane in the European Cup final when Dortmund played Juventus and, believe me, he can play. He is technically very good and is actually quite a bit taller than people imagine. He really is a great player and although it took him a while to make his presence felt for France at the World Cup in 1998, he certainly did so in some style in the final against Brazil. That was him at his best.

I remember watching Alessandro del Piero against Rangers in the Champions League a few years ago and although Alex Cleland probably won't enjoy the memory, the recollection I have is of one piece of skill from the Italian which was marvellous. It's no wonder Alex later gave him a kick and was sent off! Del Piero is a brilliant young player.

I also saw him close up in that Euro final and when he's on fire he's awesome. He produced a few moments of magic against Dortmund and threatened to turn that match for Juve but fortunately didn't manage it. We knew when he went on, though, that it would be more difficult than ever and that is a tribute to him. Even the best of the German internationals were wary.

Guys like that were obviously difficult opponents yet the man who has been the most awkward of all for me is undoubtedly Milinko Pantic. The Atletico Madrid star pulled me all over the park when Dortmund met them in the Champions League. He also nutmegged me, which was more than a bit embarrassing! Pantic could drift about the park with the minimum of fuss and bother – until, that is, it was time to do some damage and then he would step up a gear and destroy you. He was quality, and he proved it, to me at least, that night.

Two other guys I have watched and admired in the number ten jersey recently were stars of the World Cup in France – Rivaldo of Brazil and Ariel Ortega of Argentina. I played against the brilliant Brazilian in the tournament's opening game, of course, and saw for myself just how good he is. He simply never gets flustered and he always seems to have time and space. He also has a devastating left foot, as a few players at France '98 found out to their cost. Beforehand we had been led to believe that the World Cup was going to be all about Ronaldo, yet I feel it was Rivaldo who emerged from it all with more credit.

Ortega, for a few matches, was quite outstanding and was possibly the best player in the competition. He is hugely skilful and although he doesn't worry too much about defending, you allow that in his case because you know he'll cause opponents so many problems at the other end.

What you don't anticipate, admittedly, is the lack of self-control that saw him have a moment of madness against Holland when he butted Dutch goalkeeper Edwin van der Saar and was rightly sent off. That was foolish and was a massive blemish on an otherwise brilliant tournament for him. It was a pity because it's probably what he'll be remembered for from France '98 rather than some excellent football.

I have no doubt that there are lots of other players who have worn that number ten jersey and looked the part, but to me these guys were all a little bit extra-special. Something just seems to set them apart from mere mortals and it is astonishing how many very special players have worn the jersey. Ironically – or maybe just as well, in view of my last sentence – it's not a number I have worn that much at any of my clubs. Perhaps that is a good thing, though – the competition for places among that list of number tens is just too great!

10

DUMPED BY SCOTLAND

My Scotland career has come to a sudden, unexplained halt twice already so I'm desperately hoping there's not a third time for quite a while. I would like to think I have become an established international, although after previous experiences with Scotland I would never take that for granted.

I started out in the dark blue jersey as a St Mirren player way back in 1990 in a European Championship Under-21 match against Romania at Easter Road. Christian Dailly also made his debut on that occasion.

Craig Brown was in charge of the Under-21s at that time and I was honoured when he made me captain. I'm not sure why he did, other than perhaps it was because I had played in the Scottish League v. Scotland centenary game a little earlier and he had maybe seen something then that had impressed him.

I was delighted, anyway, and equally pleased when we got off to a winning start with goals from Scott Booth and

Eoin Jess. It was the beginning of a terrific campaign and we had some outstanding players during it. Apart from Jess, Booth and Dailly, others who played included Scot Gemmill, Alex Rae, Duncan Ferguson, Alex Cleland, Stevie Fulton, Michael Watt, Ray McKinnon, Billy Findlay, Paddy Connolly, Stephen Wright, Phil O'Donnell, Gerry Creaney and Alan McLaren.

I was skipper again when we met Switzerland at East End Park next time out, when Findlay scored twice and we got other goals from Connolly and Creaney in a 4–2 victory. Then we lost 2–0 in Bulgaria before another Findlay goal gave us a 1–0 win in the return leg of that fixture.

That was all enough to see us in pole position to qualify for the next phase and around the same time I recall us beating Poland and drawing with France in the Toulon tournament, so, generally speaking, we were on a bit of a roll.

When season 1991–92 came around we started off again with a 3–0 win in Switzerland – with goals from John Spencer, Creaney and Booth – and a terrific 3–1 victory away in Romania with yours truly on the scoresheet along with Creaney and Paul Bernard.

Apart from my goal, the thing I remember most about that trip was the poverty there. It was depressingly sad. At that time it was a very poor country and I will always remember that one of the Romanian players had sellotape holding his boots together. Maybe that was a good idea, though, because despite the scoreline I can assure you that they had some very good players and they gave us a bit of a doing. It was, though, my first glimpse of that kind of lifestyle and it was a humbling experience that made most of us realise how lucky we were. We might have complained a bit at that age but really we had no right to.

Anyway, that put us into the quarter-finals and I was delighted to have captained the team to some success. I stayed skipper for the next stage against Germany and we had two marvellous matches against them. The first was away and we drew 1–1, with Creaney getting the all-important goal for us. That was a very good result.

The return match at Pittodrie, however, was something else again. It was one of the greatest Under-21 matches Scotland has ever been involved in and I must say it was one of the best nights of my career. The Germans had a tremendous team which included players who were to become my team-mates at Dortmund, with Stefan Klos, Heiko Herrlich and Steffen Freund all involved in their excellent squad.

Pittodrie was packed to the rafters. The atmosphere for an Under-21 match was sensational, even if our start didn't exactly match it. We found ourselves 3–1 down – Ray McKinnon scored our goal – and therefore 4–2 in arrears on aggregate. It looked for all the world as if we were down and out and I don't think many of the players, far less the fans, would have given much for our chances at that stage.

Somehow, though, we clawed our way back into it and there were amazing scenes at Pittodrie as Creaney got one goal and then I equalised. The place was bedlam and the Germans were a bit shell-shocked because our comeback was the last thing they had expected. It was just about the last thing we had anticipated as well!

By that stage we were buzzing and there was a real feeling that we could go on and get the winner. Alex Rae duly obliged with a fantastic goal to set Pittodrie alight and I must say I had some fun when I eventually got to Dortmund by reminding Steffen, Heiko and Stefan of that result! It was one of those matches that only comes along every so often and it was great to be involved in it.

That was us through to the semis and a meeting with Sweden, although unfortunately that was where it all went wrong for me and the team. We went back to Pittodrie for the first leg and drew 0–0, which was a bit disappointing in the first place. Equally disappointing was the fact that I was taken off at half-time and replaced by Phil O'Donnell. I didn't know it at the time but it was my last act as an

Under-21 player. I wasn't picked for the return game over there, although I was on the bench, and we went on to lose 1–0 and go out of the competition.

It was a sad ending to a tremendous campaign, particularly because I felt we were a better team than the Swedes. And it was a big blow to me personally. I don't know why I was taken off in the first leg of the semis, nor do I know why I was left on the bench for the second game. Similarly, nothing was ever said to me about the captaincy. But that's football, I suppose. Players have to accept these things and coaches aren't under any obligation to give explanations. I was, nevertheless, a bit disappointed at the way it all happened and had I known then that I would be disappearing from the international scene for about three years I would have been even more upset.

I was in the wilderness as far as Scotland was concerned after that. A bit of a non-person. And that was how it stayed while I continued to do my best for Saints and then Motherwell, which are clubs never likely to attract the regular attention of international team managers.

So when I was given the call again it was, without question, out of desperation as far as Scotland was concerned. The squad was set to go to Japan for games against Ecuador and the host nation in the Kirin Cup in May 1995. A lot of big names couldn't go for one reason or another and Craig Brown had basically run out of players. He looked to Fir Park and called up Brian Martin, Rab McKinnon and myself to make up the numbers.

It would have been silly of us to look at it any other way. No one was under any illusions about why we were there and we certainly travelled more in hope than expectation. Craig Burley was also in the squad for the first time, but he certainly made a bigger impact than me. To be honest, I didn't feel particularly comfortable on the trip. That was nothing to do with anyone else, but simply a lack of confidence in my own ability. Basically, I knew I wasn't ready for the national side.

The first game was against the Japanese in Hiroshima and although I started, my experience was short-lived. John Spencer was sent off in the first half and when the team was rejigged because of that I found myself getting the big hook and being replaced by John Robertson. I don't think I got a particularly fair crack at it, but there was nothing I could do about that.

And when I didn't start against Ecuador in Toyama I knew without anyone having to tell me that it was all over. I did go on as substitute for Derek Whyte but I did wonder then if I would ever get back into the international reckoning and I had to admit to myself that the signs weren't good. I was resigned to the fact that life at that level wasn't for me. Craig Brown did say at one point that he would have a word about it all but he never did and I put the whole thing down to experience. At least I had seen a bit of Japan.

Once more that was that for some time and I know that I only returned to international football after another enforced break because I had signed for Borussia Dortmund in the interim. There's no point in beating about the bush. I don't think I would have re-entered the fray had I stayed at Motherwell. It's just a fact of life – and an understandable one really – that international bosses watch bigger clubs more than the others. As it happens, I wouldn't have minded too much if the Scotland spotlight hadn't swung towards me even at that stage because I was finding all my time being taken up trying to do well in Germany. Believe me, that was a full-time job in itself.

Anyway, by the time I was called up again Scotland were embroiled in the World Cup qualifying campaign. We had already drawn with Austria in Vienna and next up was an away double-header against Latvia and Estonia. I went on at half-time for Stuart McCall in Riga and by then we were a goal up through John Collins, even though Latvia were a decent team and had made life really difficult. In fact, it needed an unbelievable save from Andy Goram to keep us going. Andy produced the nearest thing I've ever seen to the legendary stop made by Gordon Banks to thwart Pele in the 1970 World Cup. It was an astonishing effort. Darren Jackson then went on to add a second with a superb goal and we left for Estonia convinced we would get the six points we originally set out for.

Unfortunately, things didn't quite work out the way we had planned. That trip to Tallinn has already gone down in football folklore and I must say it was an astonishing exercise by anyone's standards.

There was nothing abnormal about the preparations for the match until the night before when we were already back at our hotel after an afternoon training session. We heard then that Craig Brown and Alex Miller had been at the Kadriorg Stadium and that the floodlighting was considered to be well below the level required, but that was that. We didn't think too much more about it. Then there were lots of rumours the following day but it was really only when we reached the stadium that we began to believe that maybe the Estonians wouldn't turn up after all for a kick-off that had been brought forward from the evening to the afternoon by FIFA. They had obviously agreed with Scotland's point about the floodlighting.

Even then, though, we expected the Estonian team to appear because no one could recall another side failing to turn up, especially for a World Cup qualifying tie. So we went about our match preparations as normal and tried to shut out everything that was going on. Everyone else seemed to be doing the same thing to the point where the referee came into our dressing-room to check our studs knowing full well there was no team in the other dressing-room! Bizarre doesn't begin to describe it. It was all a bit surreal.

I had been named in the team but it was a bit difficult to concentrate because of all the nonsense going on around us. It actually reached a comical stage when we walked out to hear the Tartan Army singing 'There's only one team in Tallinn'! You couldn't argue with that.

We lined up and after John Collins and Billy Dodds touched the ball the whole ridiculous farce was brought to an end. No one knew quite what to do but I always remember with a laugh how Tosh McKinlay raised his arms in glory as if he had scored a last-gasp winner rather than simply appeared on the park for less than a minute.

We naturally believed we would be given the points and it was only later that FIFA, in their wisdom, decided that that wouldn't be the case and settled instead for another game in Monaco. When you consider that they had originally gone along with the lighting protest and had even changed the kick-off time, it was a bit of a U-turn by the game's governing body. At the time, though, it didn't bother me unduly because there was no doubt in my mind that we would beat them wherever we played.

Our thoughts then turned to Sweden at Ibrox in November. We knew that would be a huge match because even that early the group looked to be between ourselves, the Swedes and Austria. John McGinlay gave us a great start in that game but it was really Jim Leighton who helped us to a vital victory. I went on at half-time for Jackie McNamara and watched in admiration as Jim defied everything Sweden could throw at him. It was an inspired performance. We trooped off after the 1–0 victory and congratulated Jim because we all knew he had saved the day.

Then came the rearranged game against Estonia and I have to say the pitch in Tallinn would have suited us more than the one in Monaco. It was in very poor condition, although the bottom line is that there was no excuse for a 0–0 draw. I stayed on the bench on that occasion but all the players knew we should have beaten them and we left Monte Carlo knowing we had dropped two bad points. It was the type of game that Scotland should win wherever it is played and there were one or two uneasy feelings that the draw might prove costly.

The place itself, mind you, was magnificent. I could see

why Formula One drivers and top tennis stars move there, and John Collins, of course, for a spell. It was spectacular.

I was an unused substitute again next time when we had the return match against Estonia at Rugby Park. Craig Brown, though, told me I wasn't playing because I had just come up from Borussia Dortmund's Champions League game against Manchester United at Old Trafford and he obviously felt it would be better to start without me.

Scotland won convincingly enough and that finally got Estonia out of the road before we headed immediately for a Celtic Park meeting with Austria that was, once more, a key fixture in the section. I started in that one against my Borussia pal Wolfgang Feiersinger and I felt that Scotland produced possibly the best display of the group in winning 2–0. Kevin Gallacher, who had a marvellous qualifying campaign, scored both our goals and the second one especially was magnificent. There had been a bit of chat between Wolfgang and me before the game so it was nice to have the last word, although, to be fair to him, he also acknowledged that we deserved the victory.

Sweden gained some revenge for their defeat at Ibrox when they beat us 2–1 in Gothenburg and we didn't have any argument over that. They had been the better team against us twice yet we had emerged with a victory each so we couldn't really have any complaint.

We then headed into the summer with one game to go that season, against Belarus in Minsk. I joined the squad fresh from my European Cup triumph so I was on a high, but it clearly wasn't the ideal time for a fixture with most of the lads having finished quite a bit earlier. In the end we won 1–0, courtesy of a Gary McAllister penalty, on a hopeless pitch. It was a big victory for us over there and you have to hand it to Gary for having the bottle to take the spot-kick after what had happened when he'd taken one against England in the European Championships at Wembley the previous summer.

Gary takes a lot of unfair stick from Scotland fans who

don't seem to appreciate his efforts. Maybe it's because I have played alongside him that I recognise his true worth. He is a class act and that penalty deserves to be remembered just as much as the one he missed because, believe me, it was just as important.

After the break we were scheduled to meet Belarus again at Pittodrie at the beginning of September and Stephane Chapuisat and I left Stuttgart together after playing there for Dortmund. We split up in Switzerland, where he was staying for an international against Finland, and I went on to London, where I was booked into an airport hotel overnight. When I woke up the next morning I was stunned, in common with the rest of the world, at the news that was coming through about the death of Princess Diana. It was horrendous and there was a kind of unreal silence about Heathrow when I boarded a flight to Glasgow.

When I joined the squad in Aberdeen there was already a lot of talk about whether or not the game against Belarus should go ahead on the Saturday, which had already been designated as the day of the funeral. Ally McCoist, Andy Goram and Gordon Durie very quickly made their feelings known that they would have to withdraw if it went ahead and I respected their views, although they didn't necessarily coincide with mine. I would have played if the game had gone ahead that day. I'm a professional and as such I play when I'm told to play. Every player in the squad had an opinion on the matter, though, and I know for sure that some would have joined the three Rangers lads, while others would have played.

I would say, though, that it was the right decision to make when the game was put back to the Sunday. It solved the problem and also ensured the players weren't put in an awkward situation. I think everyone was as happy as they could be in the horrible circumstances.

I was rooming with Christian Dailly in Aberdeen and like the rest of the lads we watched the funeral before heading for a training session and trying to get our minds back on the business. On the Sunday we were simply glad to be playing after a difficult week and despite all the uncertainty we beat Belarus comfortably.

One way and another it was a rocky road towards France '98 and we had one more controversy before it was all over. The game that was ultimately going to decide whether or not we would make it to the World Cup finals was against Latvia and it was due to be played at Easter Road. There was an outcry about that and eventually it was switched to Celtic Park. Again it was the right decision because, with all due respect to Hibs' ground, we wanted as much backing as we could get and that meant a much bigger crowd in Glasgow.

Everything went according to plan and we won the match with a bit to spare. Austria had won the group and in theory we had to wait for Spain to beat the Faroe Islands that night before qualification was absolutely guaranteed as best second-placed nation. We celebrated as if we were through, though, that's for sure, and it's maybe just as well I didn't hear later that the Faroes had actually pulled a goal back after going 2–0 down against Spain before finally losing 3–1 to enable us to clinch our place in France.

It was a terrific achievement and all the lads were glad we didn't have to take part in the play-offs, because with teams like Italy, Russia and Belgium all involved, it would have been a bit fraught, to say the least.

The next date in the calendar was the World Cup draw in December and when I heard we were due to face Brazil in the opening match of the tournament I could hardly believe it. It was brilliant. It would have been whoever we were playing, but the fact that we were opening the whole show against the world champions made it extra special.

There was still plenty of football to be played before we thought about that, though, and although I missed a friendly against France because I had just moved to Celtic and another against Denmark through injury, I had a few minutes of a 1–1 draw against Finland.

When Craig Brown duly named his squad for a pre-World Cup trip to America he made it clear that, barring disasters, the same 22 would go to France, so I was delighted to be involved. There was no McAllister, through injury, and I felt for Gary because he had done so much to get us there. He had made it clear he was desperate for Scotland to get through to the second phase of a major competition for the first time and it must have been unbelievably sore for him to miss out.

There was also no Stuart McCall or Ally McCoist, which I was surprised about because they were good, experienced professionals and Ally especially had seemed to have given himself every chance with his form late in the season. But I don't pick the squad. I just play and from a personal point of view I was simply pleased I was going to get the chance to be at the biggest tournament of all.

First, however, was the States and let me tell you that something that happened on that trip could have put paid to Craig's best plans before we even reached France. But more of that later, and if the national manager reads this he'll probably have a heart attack!

In fact if he is anything like me when it comes to flying, he probably suffered something like that anyway on the flight from Glasgow to London on the first leg of the journey to New York. I admit I don't particularly like flying. I never have and I don't think I ever will. I treat it as a necessity and a part of my job, but that doesn't mean I have to enjoy it. Equally, I'm not quite as bad as Arsenal's Dennis Bergkamp, who has a complete phobia about it.

On that trip south, though, I could easily have developed a phobia – if I hadn't been so scared! The plane, with the players, staff, SFA personnel and journalists on board, was just about to land at Heathrow when, with just a few feet to go, the pilot pulled the aircraft back into the sky. I was petrified and I don't think I was alone. That's never happened to me before and it was not pleasant. It seemed, at least according to the explanation we received when we had all calmed down, that things weren't right in the galley at the back of the plane and that the pilot had had to abort the landing. I've had a few bad flights over the years but that went straight into my personal top ten! It was not a good start to the trip.

We did eventually make it, however, and we were based at Short Hills in New Jersey before our opening game against Colombia in New York's Giants Stadium. The hotel was very good and considering we were there for a week or so it all went pretty well. There is always the possibility of boredom creeping in on a trip like that but we trained hard, managed a bit of sunbathing and did some shopping at the mall across the road. We also went out for a couple of meals.

The first hiccup in the World Cup preparations, though, came when out of the blue the lads heard that Andy Goram was returning home. I don't know all the ins and outs of Andy's circumstances or of that decision and I don't think any of the boys even got a chance to say goodbye to him. We all respected him for doing what he felt was best but there's no doubt we were also disappointed. He has proved himself time and time again at the highest level and to have keepers of the calibre of him and Jim Leighton, as well as Neil Sullivan, was very comforting.

There was nothing anyone could do about it, however, and life goes on. When one door closes, another opens and Andy's departure gave a chance to Jonathan Gould, who was called in and arrived just in time for a game of golf and must have thought he was on his holidays!

It was a night when we all trooped into New York, though, that threatened Scotland's World Cup plans with a vengeance. Come to think of it, it probably threatened the Big Apple as well. We went in by coach with instructions to be back on board at 1 a.m. I was in a group that included John Collins, Jim Leighton, Colin Calderwood, Colin Hendry, Kevin Gallacher and Tom Boyd and we headed off for a couple of beers and a bite to eat.

We had a good night and since I had never been to New

York I discovered a bit about the city that never sleeps. That's true and it was all an experience. Did I say an experience? We eventually realised it was getting a bit late – seriously late – and we had to do something about it. So there we were, half a dozen or so of Scotland's World Cup stars, running through New York trying to get back to the coach. What we didn't expect, though, was the fact that we had to go through a fish market to get to the bus and if Craig or Alex Miller had seen their prime assets slipping and slithering about on pieces of wet fish they would have had a fit. Filleting would have been too good for us. It's a bit of a miracle that no one was injured. Just as well, too, because I don't know how we would have explained to the management team that we had been injured by a fish. Kevin had already had a food poisoning problem courtesy of a prawn earlier on the trip so that would have been some double for him.

Even then the nightmare wasn't over, because when we reached the appropriate place at a minute past one o'clock the coach had gone. Normally there is a leeway of five minutes or so when a team bus will wait for latecomers but this one didn't, and there we were stuck in the middle of New York.

I hardly have to tell you that when we jumped into two taxis, one went one way and ours went the other. Our guy was clearly lost in jig time and hadn't a clue where Short Hills was. His passengers weren't much help either. It was all enough to send John Collins apoplectic. JC was going off his head and I just hope for the sake of Merseyside taxi drivers that he doesn't have the same problem now he's at Everton!

Eventually we got the poor guy to drop us at a hotel and we ended up hiring a limo to take us back. We finally made it at around three o'clock. Then, deciding attack was the best form of defence, we gave Alex Miller some stick for letting the coach leave so quickly! But, I must admit, I don't remember mentioning the fish market episode . . .

As for the game, we drew 2–2 with Colombia and I felt we played well. We went one down to a Carlos Valderrama penalty, then Collins equalised. Craig Burley put us ahead and then when we tired in the heat late on Freddy Rincon scored for them.

I marked Valderrama most of the time and although he's getting on a bit I could see he was still a terrific player. He maybe wasn't quite as quick as he used to be but everything they did still went through him and he had a great touch.

We left the Big Apple quite pleased with the performance, which was always going to be more important than the result at that stage. After that it was off to Washington to a place called Tyson's Corner and it wasn't nearly as nice as Short Hills. In fact, it was a bit outside the city and the lads didn't see anything of the capital over the few days we were there.

Instead, we prepared for the meeting with America in the JFK Stadium, although, in truth, nothing could really have prepared us for that. The temperature in the stadium was around 100 degrees when we kicked off in the afternoon and I have never experienced anything like it. Nor do I want to again. It was insufferably hot. It was simply impossible to play at anything other than a walking pace and even the American lads, who were more used to it than us, struggled in the intense heat.

As it happened, we should have beaten them but ended up having to settle for a 0–0 draw. All through the match our substitutes sat on the sidelines with wet towels over their heads to keep them cool, but we didn't have that luxury out on the pitch. To be honest, I felt it was so hot that it was dangerous and a few of the lads were a bit unhappy about it afterwards. No one minded a bit of acclimatisation with the south of France in mind but the only way that this would have been appropriate would have been if the World Cup was being staged in the middle of the Sahara Desert!

The one good thing for me was that I managed a chat

with my wife Monica's cousin Leo, who had travelled from Alabama for the match. Even he said it was hot and, living in that State, he knows a thing or two about the heat!

We then flew straight home from Washington and despite one or two minor problems I think we all felt pretty good about the preparations for France. Generally it had all gone well. We were fit and, considering we had all had long, difficult seasons, everyone was pretty fresh. Mind you, if you can't get up for the prospect of the World Cup finals, you shouldn't be playing football. Physically and mentally we were right. We were completely focused and we all knew we had to peak in France like never before.

All that was left to do when we arrived back in Glasgow was pick up suits, shirts, ties and shoes – and the kilts we had decided to wear when we went out on to the Stade de France pitch before the opening game against Brazil. Then it was home for a couple of days and for me some precious time with my new daughter Kira, son Christopher and Monica.

11

MY FEARS IN FRANCE

There were times at the World Cup in France when I feared for my future at Celtic and, on one famous occasion in deepest downtown St Etienne, when I almost feared for my life.

One thing at a time, though, and I must admit that with a host of Celtic players at the tournament our attention was occasionally diverted by what was happening – or rather not happening – back at our club in Glasgow.

My views on the Celtic-Wim Jansen affair have been well documented elsewhere but the longer we remained without a manager or head coach, the more ludicrous it became. We heard, in common with the fans and everyone else, about a long list of supposed candidates for the job. Names ranged from Martin O'Neill of Leicester City through Carlos Alberta Perreira to Aad de Mos and back again. I think someone counted around 26 names being linked to a post that every top coach in the world should have wanted if everything was right about the club.

One name, though, kept cropping up ahead of the others and it sent a shudder of apprehension down my spine. From talking to clubmates while we were in St Remy with Scotland, I think they felt much the same way.

The man who was most prominently and regularly tipped for the job was Egil Olsen, manager of Norway, who, coincidentally, were in our World Cup group. His name was brought up so often it seemed there must be some truth in it. No smoke without fire. He was clearly the front-runner at the time. We kept in touch with all the names being bandied about because of our obvious interest and time after time we heard Olsen ahead of the rest. Hardly a day went by when he wasn't mentioned.

The news went down like the *Titanic* as far as the Celtic lads in France were concerned. We like to think we know how Celtic play the game. Traditionally, the club has always played attractive, attacking football and no one could deny that these principles were upheld most of the time during the 1997–98 season when we won the Premier League and the Coca-Cola Cup. Before that, our history is littered with glorious triumphs – Lisbon in 1967 is a perfect example – which came about whilst playing the game the way most people like to see it played. At least, the way the purists appreciate.

Mr Olsen, on the other hand, prefers to play a long-ball game and when you watch Norway perform to his style you can't possibly say they are an attractive team to look at. Let me make it clear from the outset that the manager is entitled to play whatever way he wants and, equally, no one can argue that Olsen's system hasn't proved ideal and, indeed, successful for Norway. The fact that they made it to the second phase of the World Cup and we didn't could also lead people to argue that it is better than the Scotland way of playing.

Yet I believe that would be very shortsighted. It is not proper football. Better judges of the game than me have criticised it as well and I refuse to believe it is the way forward. It is certainly not the way I like to play football and I think if you asked the rest of the Celtic lads they would agree. Craig Burley and I talked about the possibility a lot in France and we weren't exactly relishing the prospect of Olsen taking over. Someone told me that Craig wrote an article saying as much in the summer and the headline was something to do with not wanting the wally in the wellies! It's hard to argue with that.

The Norway manager's way is certainly not the Celtic way. I don't think our supporters would have taken to it readily. They know how they want the team to play. Most fans have been weaned on good football. The players, I believe, would also have been very unhappy and I have to admit I'm not sure I could have stayed at the club if Olsen had been introduced as the successor to Wim Jansen.

Mind you, after a World Cup experience in St Etienne that might have been the least of my worries! Scotland were in town to play Morocco in the last group game and the night before the match myself, Jackie McNamara and young Mark Burchill, who was with the squad, went out to get some chocolate for the lads. We wandered about for ages trying to find a shop or café, without success. It shouldn't really have been that difficult but it certainly seemed so for us.

So when a car pulled up we were quite happy and when we explained the problem the driver said he knew somewhere. We piled in and then drove for what seemed like an eternity through the streets that were, of course, unfamiliar and seemed to get darker and darker. Eventually, when I was beginning to think that a mugging was the best we could hope for, we stopped at a café. Even then, when we went in the place it was full of Moroccans! It was unbelievable. Needless to say we didn't stay long and, to be fair, the guy gave us a lift back to the hotel again. There were moments in that little saga, though, that made me wonder if we would survive intact!

I wonder how Craig Brown and Alex Miller would have

reacted to a ransom demand on the eve of a vital World
Cup tie! I don't even want to think about the answer to that
one . . .

The World Cup was, in a variety of ways, an experience.
It is a wonderful stage to play on. You are in among the
very best players the world has to offer and not many
people get that opportunity.

I loved most of it – the atmosphere, the games and all the
drama and excitement. It was good, too, to be with a group
of lads who were completely focused and determined,
albeit ultimately unsuccessful. It was just great to be part of
it all.

I have no idea at this stage if I'll still be around for the
next one in Korea and Japan in 2002. I'll be 32 then and it's
impossible to say if I'll be fit enough or playing well enough
at a high level to be considered. If everything is equal then
I would love to be there because it is the greatest
tournament in the world. But if it ended with Scotland
tomorrow I would be happy with what I have achieved at
international level. I can always say I have played at the
World Cup finals and that's certainly something to tell the
grandchildren.

There is, though, much more to the tournament, and
standing alongside the Brazil players in the Stade de France
on the outskirts of Paris, listening to 'Flower of Scotland'
and waiting to kick-start the World Cup in the sure
knowledge that the capacity 80,000 crowd is being
augmented by billions of people watching on television
around the world is one way of realising you'll never play
in such a situation again.

So it was with me on 10 June 1998. I stood and looked
around and, I must admit, I cannot imagine ever having a
prouder moment as a player. I knew there and then, more
than I had done at any other point in the build-up to the
opening game of France '98, that I was part of something
very special.

And that, of course, is what the World Cup is – a very

special tournament that attracts the greatest nations to a gathering every four years. It is a time when football seems to be a universal language around the world for a month or so.

Last summer, however, was unique for Scotland because we had never opened the show before. And for it to be against the world champions was a dream really. It was a huge privilege to be involved. It was one of those moments when you stop for a second and realise you're the envy of so many people in every corner of the globe that it was quite humbling. I have always accepted that I have been lucky throughout my career and I certainly appreciated it again then.

Yet I was ready, just as the rest of the lads were ready. We had been plotting and planning for the moment for long enough and we had had our fair share of ups and downs, laughs, disappointments and distractions along the way.

When we returned from the two-match tour to America we all realised the big show was nearly upon us. We had a couple of days at home with our families and then it was straight back down to business. The international party met up again at the Westpoint Hotel in East Kilbride on Thursday, 4 June and the first duty to be attended to was a meeting with the media. All the players went along and it seemed to go reasonably well, although in those circumstances the press lads seem to have an insatiable appetite for stories.

We then went training at Pollok's ground in Glasgow but it was a fairly straightforward session simply to get us back into the swing of things. When that was finished we had a couple of player pool matters to sort out. Our kilts, for instance, were all there waiting for us and we put them on for a photo session. Then we were all measured for golf clubs by a gentleman from the John Letters company. We were all to receive a bag and a full set of clubs. Talk about the perks of the job.

After that it was back to the business in hand. Top

Scottish referee Hugh Dallas came round to give us a talk on what we could expect from officials in France. Hugh had been selected to go to France '98 and as such had had an earlier briefing from FIFA. The players listened intently to Hugh – there's a first! – and also watched a video nasty on the kind of tackling that would incur the wrath of referees during the tournament.

One of the tackles we saw, by Feyenoord's Bosvelt on Denis Irwin of Manchester United, was a shocker. It was the first time I had seen it and I cringed. No wonder there had been such controversy about that moment. Generally, players realise that the tackle from behind is dangerous and there was no two ways about it – seeing that video certainly reinforced the view.

The lads then had the option to go home for the night if they wanted. The players from further afield all stayed in East Kilbride but I went back to the family for what I knew would be the last night for some time. We then all met up again at Pollok on the Friday morning for another training session before heading for the airport and the flight to Marseilles.

The French certainly looked after the competing teams because we were whisked straight off the plane and on to a coach for the trip to our headquarters just outside St Remy, and when we arrived everyone seemed quite happy with the arrangements.

That all changed, though, when we had our photographs taken for the World Cup accreditations. Honestly, I don't know how the photographer did it – on second thoughts, maybe he didn't have to try that hard! – but we all ended up looking like refugees from Chernobyl. Some of the sights weren't for the fainthearted.

Jackie McNamara and Simon Donnelly took one look at Craig Burley's picture, for example, and thought they had put an old photo of Alan Stubbs in instead! Not that Sid had anything to laugh about, because his photo would certainly have ruined his reputation if the fans at home had been given the opportunity to see it. He would never have been able to show his face again. Gordon Durie didn't exactly look a picture of health on his either, and big Matt Elliott ended up with a head the size of a pea in his.

It all gave the lads a good laugh and pride of place – if that's the right expression – went to skipper Colin Hendry. His was a disaster. We thought he would use his captain's armband to cover it up.

The rest of the day was spent recovering from that and settling into our new surroundings which, unlike some hotels where I have stayed with teams in the past, were greeted with universal approval. I was rooming with Craig Burley. He had bought a CD player during the trip to the States and we had both picked up some CDs at Glasgow Airport so it was home from home pretty quickly.

Rooming with Craig is an experience. He's a great lad but sleeps for Scotland. Rip Van Winkle has nothing on him. Every morning we were in France we went through the same routine. I always got up at nine o'clock and always asked Craig if he was going down to breakfast. Every day the question was the same and every day so was the answer. He would grunt, turn over and go back to sleep. He didn't make breakfast once. I wouldn't have minded, but it meant I had to pick up his training gear for him every day and in the end I felt like his servant. How the other half live!

As for the work side of things, we trained daily and sometimes twice a day at the local stadium, which was first class. Generally there was a decent crowd there to watch us go through our routines but later on, maybe around five o'clock, John Collins, Craig, Kevin Gallacher, Billy McKinlay and a couple of others would go back down and practise free-kicks away from everyone and from prying eyes. You just never know who is watching. Throughout it all the weather was brilliant and that certainly suited some of the lads who spent whatever spare time we had down by the side of the pool.

So generally things were going along quite nicely. Craig Brown and Alex Miller gradually started to introduce us to details about Brazil and as we watched videos of them in action there's no doubt we were completely focused. We were also, believe it or not, quietly confident.

Personally, I was by then convinced that there was no chance of us being turned over as some people were suggesting. The two games in the US had proved to me beyond all doubt that we had players who could keep the ball and play in the heat, which was going to be important when we faced the defending world champions.

Craig and Alex told us the team on the Monday and I suppose there were a couple of surprises. I think quite a few people had expected Craig to be moved from his normal international wing-back role into his more favoured midfield beat but it was Scotland business as usual for him. And one or two eyebrows were raised at Darren Jackson's inclusion just behind Gallacher and Durie. It was as attacking a line-up as anyone could possibly have envisaged.

The players seemed happy with it, though, and the mood was good when we left for Paris on the Tuesday morning before the match on the Wednesday afternoon.

It was the strangest thing, really. Up until we reached Paris we had been pretty isolated from all the hype and buzz. We took turns at going to meet the media at a local primary school in St Remy but by and large you almost wouldn't have known the World Cup opening match was just around the corner.

We certainly did when we reached the capital, however. Security, which had been very tight at our St Remy base, was incredible. Everywhere you looked there were police or army with machine-guns and clearly they were leaving nothing to chance. Once again, we were whisked straight from the plane to the coach and taken to the Stade de France, where we were going to have our statutory training session out on the pitch.

The stadium, as you might expect for one that was purpose-built for the finals, was pretty impressive. The dressing-rooms were awesome and generally everything seemed first class. When we walked out on to the pitch and as I had a look around, the thing that struck me most was the size of the press box. It seemed to take up most of the main stand.

The session itself was fairly light-hearted and not too strenuous. The hard work had all been done by then and, besides, you never knew who might be watching from the stands, ready to pick up on something. As it happened, I think the lads would have played Brazil there and then because we felt ready and couldn't wait for the action to begin.

But there were another 24 hours to go so we headed off to our hotel about half an hour from the stadium and checked in. It's a minor point and made no real difference but it was disappointing to find that we weren't the only people in it. We had completely taken over the St Remy hotel and that was great. There were no 'outsiders'. Yet people were milling about the Paris hotel and it was a slight distraction.

Funnily enough, Murdo MacLeod was staying there too. He was on Scottish Football Association business and he mentioned to me that he was meeting Wim Jansen later on. I have stressed elsewhere how much I respect Wim for what he had done with us the previous season so I was delighted to go with Craig Burley and Jonathan Gould for a chat with him. He never changes and it was great to see him again because when he had left Celtic everything had been fairly acrimonious between him and the club.

We had another visitor to the hotel too – Tony Blair. The Prime Minister came to see us and he seemed like a decent guy. He stayed and chatted with all the lads for quite a while, and either he was genuinely interested in football or he had done his homework because when Craig Brown introduced me to him he asked me how much I had enjoyed my time in Dortmund. Maybe it was just a politician's clever touch but it worked, and he didn't seem to have any airs or graces about him.

Meanwhile, word continued to filter back to us from the Brazil camp, where it seemed their manager Mario Zagallo had had some unkind things to say about Scotland in the days leading up to the opening game. I must say I don't pay too much attention to that kind of thing although it does wind some players up when they hear other managers allegedly saying they can't play or are too tough or whatever. I'm never wholly convinced about it. Someone as professional as Zagallo – who, after all, has won the World Cup as a player and as a manager – doesn't strike me as the type to demean his fellow professionals. Even if he had done, though, I wouldn't have paid any attention. It would have been water off a duck's back to me. I had faith in Scotland and the guys I was playing alongside and he could have said we were a pub team for all I was concerned. Like I say, we were focused.

All of it, though, added to the sense of occasion. The players went to bed realising more than ever before the significance of the match coming up. I know I went to sleep thinking that whatever had happened before – European Cup final included – and whatever might happen in the future I would never play in a game watched by more people.

When the great day dawned, at least one thing didn't change. Burley still slept. But with a five o'clock kick-off and the fact that we had to be at the Stade de France well in advance because of the opening ceremony, there wasn't a lot more we could do. It was a lazy day. The calm before the storm, if you like.

When the moment to leave arrived, we were an impressive sight all decked out in the full tartan regalia. I don't suppose it scared the Brazilians but it certainly gave me a fright!

Seriously, though, I think we felt pretty good about it all

and as we made our way through the crowds lining the way to the Stade de France, the prospect of what lay ahead became more and more real. At the ground we received a rapturous reception from the Scotland fans – and, for that matter, the Brazilian supporters. The two countries have always had a good relationship where football is concerned and they all took a shine to our dress sense.

We wandered about the pitch for a while, getting a feel of the atmosphere, and most of the lads took the chance to go over to the corner of the ground where we hoped to spot family and friends we had given tickets to. Monica, Christopher and my mum and dad were there but I only spotted dad. They had had my complimentary tickets and from the allocation I had been allowed to buy I had given two to Wim Jansen and one to Celtic team-mate Malky Mackay, although I didn't see them inside the stadium.

As we walked back off the pitch and up the tunnel to the dressing-room I saw Edmundo but he was the only Brazil player I encountered until we met up again as we made our way on to the park for the main event.

The two dressing-rooms were a fair way apart and more or less doubled as the warm-up areas which, in the circumstances, wasn't ideal. The opening ceremony meant that we couldn't do anything out on the pitch and instead both ourselves and the Brazilians were confined to what amounted to big rooms. It was faintly bizarre, bearing in mind the magnitude of the match.

As the clock ticked onwards, our dressing-room was quiet. Most of the guys were busy doing their own thing. Jim Leighton went into what I presume is his routine at Aberdeen and didn't get disturbed. I went about my business as well and didn't say much to anyone.

Craig Brown and Alex Miller moved among the lads, giving last-minute instructions and making points, but the overall impression for anyone who had wandered in would have been that it was a bit like a library. There was no shouting or bawling. No dramas. Just a group of professionals preparing in what they thought was the right way.

When the time came to go it was slightly different. Shouts of 'Come on' were heard and everyone went round wishing everyone else luck. The spirit was good. The determination was ferocious. The desire was very apparent.

The two teams approached the Stade de France tunnel from different directions and met up for the first time there. I make a point of not looking at the opposition whoever it is – although there has been the odd exception – so I didn't change for that game. I see no reason to try and out-stare the opposition or make any eye contact at all. I don't see what purpose that serves and I'm not interested in doing it.

What we knew, though, is that we were about to play a quality team. They were the world champions and had some exceptionally gifted individuals. The main man, at least in the vast pre-World Cup hype, was Ronaldo but they had other fine players too, like Roberto Carlos, Dunga and Rivaldo.

Indeed, I knew if I had to come up against anyone in particular it would probably be Rivaldo. There had been no specific instructions from Craig Brown about that – nor, indeed, to anyone to man-mark Ronaldo – but having watched videos I knew I would be in the same area of the pitch as Rivaldo a fair amount of the time.

It was when I heard 'Flower of Scotland' that the magnitude of the occasion fully dawned on me. I cannot imagine I will ever experience another international moment like that. It may sound a bit corny but I actually like that tune and, believe me, in those circumstances it was a bit special.

It was one of those moments that will live with me forever. Remember, there were only 11 Scots out there on the pitch experiencing it and as I've pointed out before nothing quite like it is ever likely to happen again. It was, in every sense, a once-in-a-lifetime experience and I don't think I will ever be more proud to be a Scot than I was in those few minutes in the Stade de France.

If those few moments were wonderful, then the next few were unforgettable for all the wrong reasons. We had a hell of a start to the game. We had talked beforehand about the need for a good opening spell but the masterplan was ripped up after just five minutes. Brazil scored through a Cesar Sampaio header from a corner and apart from it being a bad goal to lose at any time, it was a disastrous one to lose in the opening stages of the first World Cup game against the champions. It was also an uncharacteristic goal for Scotland to lose because we had qualified for France on the back of an outstanding defensive record as much as anything else.

I suppose people watching around the world, including back home in Scotland, must have sat back then and feared the worst. I guess millions of folk felt we were facing a mauling at that stage. And for the next ten minutes or so there was little to suggest otherwise. Dunga was pulling all the strings for Brazil and everything that mattered was going through him, with us seemingly incapable of doing anything about it. We were being pulled about all over the Stade de France and it was not pleasant.

Yet we never lost our heads. Sure, it was difficult, but none of the lads retreated into a shell after that disastrous opening and instead we played our way back into the match in what I would like to believe was some style. We got to grips with proceedings and that reinforced our view that Brazil were by no means unbeatable because they looked less than comfortable as we pushed the ball about purposefully.

It was no surprise, then, when we equalised near half-time through a John Collins penalty after a push on Kevin Gallacher. From our point of view it looked a certain spot-kick, although I have to admit if I had been a Brazilian I would have thought the decision was a bit tough. We were happy enough, though, and it made a change for us to get a wee break.

Everyone knew that John would take the penalty and we were comfortable with that. He's an excellent player and strikes a good dead ball. I was confident he would score and when he did I looked over to the Scotland fans, who were going absolutely potty. On the pitch the lads were saying to each other to keep playing and not to lose concentration, which can sometimes happen after a goal.

At that point the worst scenario as far as I was concerned was a draw, but then fate took a hand – and that is a familiar call for Scotland. The ball that bounced off Tom Boyd's shoulder and went into our net could have hit my clubmate anywhere else and wouldn't have gone in. It was incredibly bad luck and salt was rubbed into our wounds when we thought back to a few seconds previously when a similar ball had gone inches the wrong side of the post at the other end. Talk about sod's law.

To be fair, with Denilson on for Bebeto the Brazilians did look a better team, but even so we had a late chance through a Collins free-kick that undoubtedly struck Dunga's hand. I don't think too many people saw it – the referee certainly didn't! – but there again I don't think we would have been awarded a second spot-kick anyway. That would have been a bit much to expect in the circumstances.

Looking back at it now, I often wonder what would have happened if we had gone 2–1 up instead of them. It would have been interesting to see how they reacted because I had felt they were there for the taking at 1–1.

But bad luck follows us about and, anyway, I hate hard-luck stories. We lost and there was nothing we could do about it, although there was a small degree of consolation in the way we played. It was, though, still really disap-pointing to come away from Paris with nothing to show for our efforts apart from, in my case, Rivaldo's jersey.

After the game my family had to dash away immedi-ately to catch flights home but the rest of the lads had a chance to see wives or girlfriends, and they enjoyed the opportunity. We flew straight 'home' ourselves after that and although the lads reflected on the result and everything to do with it, we knew we couldn't change it and that it was an opportunity missed, which was frustrating.

We were, however, soon back in the old routine of one or two training sessions a day, although on the Friday night we had a break when we went to Marseilles to watch France against South Africa at the Velodrome. I enjoyed it and I have to admit to being a fan of the French national anthem. It created a great atmosphere that night and with over 55,000 in the ground it was the place to be. It certainly put one or two of our squad in the mood. We ran a sweep among the lads for first goal scored, first booking and so on and when Darren Jackson and Billy McKinlay won some cash they were despatched to buy the guys some food. We couldn't believe it when they returned with the grub – and their faces painted in the red, white and blue of France!

We had one other interesting night between the game against Brazil and the next one against Norway in Bordeaux. Masseur Stewart McMillan picked a restaurant for us all in St Remy and boasted that it was the best one in town. I hardly need to tell you that within minutes of us sitting down it became known as Restaurant Diabolique. The service was bad and the food worse. I didn't think it would be easy to find a bad restaurant in St Remy but Stewart managed it and took some stick on the strength of it. In fact, the lads threatened to throw him into the swimming pool back at the hotel, which perhaps explains why he wasn't seen again for the rest of the trip.

Other than that, the spare time was spent relaxing by the pool, going down into the town for a coffee, playing pool or simply watching the other World Cup matches on television. Some of the lads managed a game of golf as well and Darren wanted to organise a high-diving contest but he was given short shrift. I was surprised at him wanting to do something so active, because up until then he had been content with browning himself under the sun. He rotated so much there were times I'm sure he was on a spit.

On the business front, we watched Norway on video when they beat Brazil 4–2 in a friendly and also when they drew 2–2 with Morocco in their opening section match. I was interested in them because I knew a couple of the lads from my time in Germany. Havard Flo was at Werder Bremen and Kjetil Rekdal was at Hertha Berlin so I had played against them before.

We flew to Bordeaux knowing we could use a victory and when we trained on the pitch at the Stade Lescure we knew we could have no excuses when the time came. It was like a bowling green. Craig Brown also named a same-again team and we felt we were ready for the Norwegians.

When the time came we murdered them – and yet ended up with a 1–1 draw. It was criminal. We played all the football and Norway didn't. I know that Olsen likes their style but I really, really don't and that was confirmed during the match. It's horrible to play against and, I would imagine, pretty awful to watch.

We should have been two goals ahead by half-time, we were so far in front, but the fact that we weren't always made it a bit fraught. Sure enough, just after the interval Flo scored with a terrible goal from our point of view and once more we were faced with trying to salvage something from behind. It seemed to be the story of our lives.

We needed a break, and we got one – even if it wasn't the kind we wanted! Colin Calderwood's hand was broken and he was replaced by David Weir. Then, a few minutes later, Jackie McNamara went on for Darren, with Craig moving into midfield. The net result of all that was a terrific equaliser from Craig, who latched on to a great ball from David and scored a superb goal.

That was it, unfortunately, and the Norwegians cele-brated because they knew they had got out of jail. I doubt if they have ever come away with that kind of result after being so comprehensively outplayed and, naturally, we were a bit upset.

The one bright spot of the day was Brazil's impressive

3–0 win over Morocco because that ensured we still had something to play for in the last match. If that hadn't been the case it would have been a very long last week. It would have been very difficult indeed.

Instead it was a long night as we headed back to St Remy even though we remained optimistic about our chances. We knew we could have had four points in the bag rather than just one, but the fact we were still in there with a chance helped.

Back at base camp it was really more of the same. We had a pool competition, with Craig and I seeing off the youngsters in the shape of Jackie McNamara and Simon Donnelly, and it has to be said they might not grow old if they don't pay their dues soon! I can't believe they haven't paid yet.

We had another night in St Remy as well and it was then that Craig decided to do his Marilyn Monroe imperson- ation and go blond. Jonathan Gould and Sid also said they would get the bleached look but I think they thought twice about it when they sobered up! Not so Burley. He went ahead with it the next day at a local hairdresser and turned up just in time for a team meeting at five o'clock when, I think it's fair to say, he took a bit of stick.

We also had a reception at the town hall when we all signed their visitors' book and met the mayor. A host of local kids, who had obviously spent hours rehearsing, then gave us a good rendition of 'Flower of Scotland' and we appreciated the time and effort they must have put in to get it right.

So the time passed reasonably quickly and the count- down was on to Morocco in St Etienne, where we knew it was basically win or bust. We trained at the Stade Geoffroy-Guichard as usual the night before the match and I have to say I wasn't impressed. The pitch was poor and it was so slippery the lads were left wondering whether to wear studs or moulds for footwear. Maybe I should have got the vibes there and then.

As it was, I knew the Moroccans would be dangerous opponents. I suspected that because these teams always are. No one knew too much about them and that made me wary, maybe even more so than before we faced Brazil or Norway because we had known what we were getting into with them. Even after Craig had gone over everything I was a bit uneasy.

As it turned out, I was right to be concerned. They were an excellent side and we simply never got going. It just never happened for us on the night, although you have to give some credit to them for that. The old saying about only playing as well as you're allowed to springs to mind.

We again lost bad goals and when Craig was sent off any slim chance we had of recovery – and it was slim at best by then – disappeared. I thought he was a bit unlucky because at first it seemed as if the referee was going to flash his yellow card. Then he was surrounded by Moroccans and produced red instead!

The game was going away from us by then anyway and in truth we could have ended up even worse off than 3–0. We were chasing shadows by the end of the night and nothing good came from it. Basically, on the night, we weren't good enough and that hurt.

Morocco clearly felt they had done enough to go through and you couldn't blame them for that. They danced about, swapped shirts happily – I exchanged with Bassir, who had scored twice – and it looked as if they had won the World Cup itself. Then the roof fell in on them. News filtered through that Norway had, incredibly, beaten Brazil 2–1 in Marseilles to pip the Moroccans for a place in the second phase. At first they couldn't believe it – understandably – and then it sunk in. It was astonishing how they went from a massive high to an all-time low in just a couple of minutes and you had to feel for them.

I personally would have preferred Morocco to have gone through if it couldn't have been us. They at least play the game the way it should be played and I felt they deserved it more than Norway.

As for us, we were down and out of the World Cup. Normally we would have sat in the dressing-room with our heads in our hands but on this occasion we felt we owed it to the fans to go out and take some sort of bow.

I must admit I'm not a great believer in celebrating – if that's the right word – failure, and ultimately that was what it was. We had taken just one point from a possible nine, in the draw with the Norwegians, and it wasn't a lot to show. Yet in two of the matches we had played pretty well and I think the supporters who packed the Geoffroy-Guichard Stadium that night recognised that fact.

They had been absolutely brilliant throughout. Wherever we went we were cheered long and loud and the backing they gave the team was the envy of every other country. The Tartan Army probably has its faults but on the whole they travel to follow Scotland intent only on having a good time, having a few beers and generally partying, as well as watching football. Some other countries can't say that.

Unfortunately fans don't win you games and trophies out on the pitch and we were left with the old Scottish hard-luck story. I had said before we went to France that I didn't want to know about that kind of thing but that's what we ended up with nevertheless.

As far as my own performances were concerned, I don't really care. When I say that I mean that I don't analyse them afterwards. That's for other people to do. If I had felt out of my depth in the three matches in France, though, I would have been very disappointed.

In all honesty, however, I am concerned only about the team. People may not believe that but I have learned over the years that individuals can't win things on their own. They can help, of course, but it has to be a team effort. You stand or fall together. That is the only way. And, ultimately, you can't change a thing when it's over. There will always be ifs and buts and maybes but so what? When the final whistle blows, you've had your chance. If you've taken it, great; if you haven't, tough.

We were left thinking only about going home and that meant leaving the St Remy hotel where everyone had looked after us so well. I even made friends with one of the security guys assigned to protect the Scotland party while it was in France. These lads were brilliant. They were never too far from our side – apart from in St Etienne! – and I was fascinated by their lifestyle.

I was astonished at the level of security that was around us generally but that was the way the tournament organisers wanted it. I suppose it's better to be safe than sorry in this day and age, although some of the media lads who went to see the Moroccans before our match said they were operating an open house! Their players wandered about and there wasn't a security guy in sight, apparently.

Mind you, they didn't always have to be in sight. I remember walking into St Remy for a coffee with a few of the lads and we noticed one of our security people about 20 yards behind. When we sat down at the café he seemed to have disappeared so we assumed he had gone back to the hotel. When we got up to pay, though, he appeared seemingly from nowhere and tailed us back again!

It was only really before the game in Bordeaux that I got to know them. One big guy called Paco who didn't say much was nicknamed Wesley Snipes, and then there was Ritchie and Dominic. They were the lads I ended up talking to. I spoke a lot to Dominic in particular because I was intrigued by their jobs, how they went about it and what they got up to. He actually showed me into his room one day and I couldn't believe it. The place was like the flight deck of the Starship Enterprise. There were computers and gadgets everywhere. His machine-gun was there and I even spotted a grenade.

He had already shown me the pistol the security guys carried with them at all times and I had thought that was impressive enough but we are talking here about a mini armoury in his room. I wanted a go with the guns but there was nowhere suitable nearby – which was probably just as well from the locals' point of view!

He did say, though, that he would show me round his unit in Paris and let me try the weapons there if I was ever in the capital. In fact, what he actually said was that if I was ever there and didn't look him up he would kill me himself! He might not have meant that but, I can tell you, he seemed very capable of looking after himself. They all did. I don't think they would have taken too kindly to being messed about by anyone.

They told me they had had a spell in the Congo which hadn't been too much of a picnic. They said that it had been a bit dodgy and that they had had their lives in their hands a few times over there. I didn't doubt it for a second. When they had finished guarding us some of them were moving on to one of the other World Cup countries and then heading for Algeria. It was, to say the least, an interesting life.

I joked with them at one point that looking after Scotland must have been one of their cushiest jobs and up to a point they agreed. But they also insisted that it had had its difficulties and one, believe it or not, was when the fans were around the areas we were staying. Scotland supporters inevitably wear the official strip and sometimes, they said, it was confusing for them if fans and players were together!

They all followed us right to the steps of the plane home to make sure we were safely on our way and if I get the opportunity I will go to Paris and see Dominic because I would be interested to see more of how they operate.

When we arrived back in Scotland we were amazed at the scenes at Glasgow Airport. Hundreds of fans were there to greet us and the thought ran through my head about what it would be like if we ever really achieved anything.

It must be said that we didn't at France '98 but there were plenty who did. France seemed to be worthy winners. They caught Brazil in the final at a good time, in view of the anxieties surrounding Ronaldo, and unlike us took full advantage. Even then, I don't think anyone would have forecast a 3-0 win. Good luck to them, though. Paris and the rest of the country went crazy and there are probably still a few hangovers being nursed. As for the supporters . . .!

Looking back at the tournament now, I think it was a pretty good World Cup. There were problems, as there always will be at such a huge event, and the authorities may have to look at the length of the whole thing. It was on for a month and, as we have seen, that doesn't leave too much time for players to recover before the start of the new season in Europe at least.

Another problem can be resolved by players themselves. It has become a source of concern – quite rightly – that players diving and feigning injury to get something for their team or to get an opponent into trouble was very much in evidence in France. I hate that. I would much rather find out if I'm good enough or not by simply playing the game and I think most British players are like that. It is a bit different in some parts of the continent – and, for that matter, on other continents – and FIFA will have to look at it carefully before it becomes an even more serious problem. There is no room in football for that kind of nonsense.

On the plus side, I felt there was a lot of good football played and there were certainly some outstanding players. Dennis Bergkamp did well for Holland, Lilian Thuram was terrific for France and England's Michael Owen is clearly a bit special. He scored one of the goals of the tournament and looks to have a great future. I have played against him for Celtic and I can confirm he has sensational pace. The sky is the limit for him when he picks up a bit more experience and game awareness.

But three players in particular stood out for me from all the football I watched during the summer: Rivaldo, Zinedine Zidane and Edgar Davids. I saw only the Brazilian at close quarters – really close quarters! – and he is special. Ronaldo takes most of the spotlight in their squad and he has very quick feet but for me Rivaldo is their main man. He certainly was in France. He is just so aware and intelligent. Maybe he's helped by the focus being entirely on his team-mate, but he has quality written all over him. I was hugely impressed.

The Frenchman went into the tournament with a massive responsibility resting on his shoulders because the whole of France expected him to produce miracles. Astonishingly, he did when it mattered most. Zidane was relatively quiet to start with and was sent off in the early stages, which caused a bit of a fuss, but he bounced back in some style. And when he had to deliver – in the final against Brazil – he did just that. He scored twice with headers which has never been recognised as the strongest part of his game and looked every inch the player we know he is. I even saw him smile afterwards!

Yet for me the outstanding player was the Dutchman. Every time I saw Holland he was immense. He seemed to be running the show for them and when you look around at the quality they have in their team that says something. Everything that mattered went through him and he looked like a man possessed. I don't know if he was trying to prove a point or not, but if he was he was certainly successful. He was sent home, remember, from Euro '96 in England but later patched up his differences and Holland reaped the benefit at the World Cup. He was the complete midfield man.

Now his performances and the whole show have been consigned to the history books and we have to look forward to the European Championships of 2000 and beyond. We have already started our qualifying campaign with Craig Brown and Alex Miller at the helm once more. The two work well together. If they have a particular strength it is their organisation and, if you like, their thoroughness. The players are well looked after and nothing is left to chance.

I must admit, I think it is an incredibly difficult job. It's not like being a club manager, who can give you a roasting and then sort things out at the training ground the next day or in the next match a few days later. Craig and Alex don't have that luxury. Scotland will play an international and an hour after the final whistle the players will disappear from their presence, if not from their thoughts, for perhaps a couple of months. It must be hard to maintain the continuity, but to be fair to them both there has in my time always been a bit of the club spirit about the Scotland squad.

New players are coming through now as well but I was interested to read Craig after the World Cup pointing out that there wouldn't be wholesale changes. It's good – vital, even – that other players are pushing for international places and some will undoubtedly be successful. Others, though, will find it difficult because there is a huge gap between playing for your club and playing for your country. It is a quantum leap. Individual players and teams are more aware and technically superior and it is an altogether different level.

We'll find out just how successful we are as we move on from the World Cup to the European Championships.

12

SCOTTISH FOOTBALL, DREAM TEAMS AND HOBBY-HORSES

Maybe I was spoiled by having some time in the Bundesliga in Germany because a lot of things there, in a football sense, seem so much better than they are here and I have to say the new-style Scottish Premier League missed a huge opportunity when the set-up was changed recently. The powers that be tinkered with the system when they had a real opportunity to overhaul it and make wholesale alterations.

We have our names and numbers on the backs of our shirts (big deal), we have a couple of youngsters on the bench at league games and we have a short winter break, along with various other odds and ends. But if you had taken a poll of the country's players you would have found that one of the main items they wanted changed was the situation where we play each other four times a season.

I wouldn't imagine there is another country in the top

levels of the game where that happens. It certainly doesn't, for instance, in Italy, Germany, France or England, which are all recognised as being among the élite leagues in Europe. So why Scotland? Part of the answer, of course, is that other clubs like two home games against Celtic and Rangers. They are the biggest money-spinners of the season and that is a powerful argument, from their point of view at least, for keeping things the way they are. Yet in the 1997–98 season we ended up playing Dundee United six times. We even played them in back-to-back matches on two separate occasions. I knew their players better than I knew my next-door neighbours! It was ridiculous, yet some of the people who make the decisions still wonder why the quality of football isn't always that great. Familiarity breeds contempt or, in this case, staleness. It shouldn't take a rocket scientist to work that out.

Six times in one season was nonsense, four times would have been plain daft and twice – plus maybe a cup-tie – would surely be more sensible. I can't speak for every player in the country but the ones I have talked to about it would also prefer just the two games. Mind you, as I've said elsewhere, we're only players. I am not aware of players having been consulted at any stage when the new Scottish Premier League was being discussed in board-rooms around the country, and chairmen and directors will no doubt say that that is how it should be, but they're not out there where it really matters.

I would like to see 16 teams in the top division playing each other twice and I believe there are now enough ambitious clubs in this country to warrant that. The set-up would include the current top ten plus others like Airdrie, St Mirren, Hibs, Falkirk (if they get a new stadium), Raith Rovers and Morton, and maybe even Livingston and Inverness Caley Thistle would be in with a shout.

While I'm on my hobby-horse – and I know that this will touch a nerve with some – why not get some of the smaller clubs to amalgamate? That way we would definitely have enough teams who could compete at a decent level with proper grounds and everything else that is required.

I will never understand, for instance, how Scotland can keep 40 senior clubs going. England has 92 – just over twice the number – yet the population is roughly ten times that of this country. Where is the logic in that? I often wonder how they all survive and it's a bit of a miracle that the last to go out of business was Third Lanark, whom a whole genera-tion of fans have probably never even heard of. Others have certainly gone close to dying. You could argue that the old Meadowbank Thistle, which is now Livingston, was one and both Partick Thistle and Falkirk diced with death just last season.

So, maybe a bit of merging is the answer. There are clubs dotted throughout the country in close proximity to others who could get their acts together so much more impres-sively if they were to join forces. There would be a lot of flak, of course, and a variety of obstacles would need to be surmounted, but that's the way of the world.

Supporters of these teams would complain about loss of identity, yet how many actually attend their club's matches? You see the attendances in the Sunday newspapers and there are all sorts of games that regularly attract just 200 or 300 people. Others would inevitably come out of the woodwork if their club was under threat, but where are they the rest of the time when it matters, week in, week out? They can't have it every way. Nothing comes easy and change is sometimes painful. But if it's merge or die, I would have thought the former option was the preferable one.

I genuinely wonder how much longer some of our clubs will be able to keep going in this day and age, and rather than them being lost altogether, surely it would be better, from both the economic and the football point of view, to get together with a neighbour?

If all that happened, perhaps we would get better facilities as well. I'm reluctant to keep harping back to Germany but clubs there all have better training facilities than any in this country – and I include Celtic and Rangers in that. It's unbelievable that the Old Firm are still not up to scratch with proper training grounds of their own. Celtic have Barrowfield, of course, but it isn't exactly state of the art. Rangers, meanwhile, have only just recently bought a ground.

Yet clubs abroad have had these facilities for probably more than a decade. I remember going on pre-season trips years ago and marvelling at the grounds and facilities some of the smaller clubs had, never mind the top teams. They had training pitches, indoor halls and every conceivable facility that would both encourage youngsters and help established players. We are only now getting around to playing catch-up – which is a bit of an indictment of clubs in this country who like to think of themselves as big-time.

Back on this season's reorganisation front, it was interesting to see that there will now be a mid-winter break in Scotland. We had one in Germany which, by and large, was successful. It's impossible to get the timing right every year, but we finished around the first week of December and didn't start playing again until 14 February. The players had a month off when foreigners would head home and local lads would go on holiday before returning for a mini pre-season. We then had a week in Dortmund and maybe ten days in Portugal before we started again. It was a long break.

The weather in Germany is not much different from that here yet, in contrast, the new plans mean we will only have a three-week stoppage. When it comes to the crunch, it will hardly be a break at all. Players might get up to a week off but then they'll be expected to begin training again to be ready for a fortnight's time. The best I can say about it, I suppose, is that something is better than nothing. I know I will be accused of thinking I'm an expert on everything but although I'm quite sure there are football matters that aren't perfect in Germany, they do seem to be ahead of us in so many ways.

Every Bundesliga stadium, for example, is pretty impressive. Borussia's Westfalen, where I played, is incredible and now they have put in under-soil heating too and are building a new section on top of the old south tribune, which is the equivalent of Celtic's old Jungle. The capacity will go up to 70,000 when the work is completed.

That ground will always have a special place in my heart for obvious reasons, although when I was playing there regularly I can assure you I didn't know there was an old wartime bomb underneath the pitch. Workmen discovered that in the summer and I heard about it when I was at the World Cup with Scotland. I must say a shiver ran down my spine at the news. I never did hear how much of a threat it ever was but the fact that it was there at all was enough for me!

When you're talking about an impressive stadium like Westfalen, though, it has to be said that they don't come much better than Celtic Park. You can say what you like about managing director Fergus McCann – and people tend to – but he deserves enormous credit for what he has achieved with the stadium. The place has been transformed and now it is a spectacular arena in which to play football.

Funnily enough, there is a close affinity between Celtic and Dortmund because the clubs have met a couple of times in the past and when I was in Germany I could regularly see Celtic scarves in amongst the crowd. Now the two grounds must be among the best in Europe.

There are other grounds I have enjoyed playing at over the years – and some more I have hated with a passion. My other favourites include Atletico Madrid's Vicente Calderon Stadium, Stuttgart's Gottlieb-Daimler Stadium, Manchester United's Old Trafford, the Olympic Stadium in Munich and the Stade de France. That's a magnificent seven, along with Westfalen and Celtic Park.

I played in Madrid during Dortmund's brilliant Champions League run and the atmosphere was electric. It was a great night and it was one of those occasions you remember as a player. Games and grounds come and go but the Vicente Calderon is special.

Stuttgart was similar in a lot of ways. It was a big game for Dortmund and again the atmosphere was special. But the whole stadium was impressive. Just like Old Trafford, in fact. United's ground is right up there among the best as well and although I didn't see all round the place I would imagine it is just as good behind the scenes as it is looking from the pitch.

The ground in Munich will always be special to me because of playing there in the European Cup final but even before that I enjoyed playing there against Bayern Munich, while the magnificent Stade de France, where Scotland opened the World Cup against Brazil in the summer, is spectacular.

Of course, for every ground I have really enjoyed playing at there are others where I have never felt really comfortable and where, to be honest, I would be quite happy never to go back to. In some cases that wouldn't be possible anyway.

Possibly the worst from my point of view was Kilbowie. The good news for me, at least, is that the home of Clydebank has gone and I can't say I'm sorry. I really didn't enjoy the few times I played there. The one major memory is of the old social club that sat in a corner of the ground but overall it was a ground I never liked visiting.

I suppose Douglas Park was much the same. Hamilton's ground is another that has bitten the dust – or at least been reduced to dust – and again I haven't lost any sleep about that. The atmosphere, such as it was, was always a bit unreal there and the pitch had a slope on it, which didn't help much. It certainly wasn't the Olympic Stadium, that's for sure!

Brechin's Glebe Park was one of these places where it somehow never felt quite right to be playing football. It's a while since I've been there, but certainly at one time there was a hedge running along the side of the ground and that never seemed quite appropriate.

Still in Scotland, Brockville remains on the go but, from all accounts, only just. When I was last there it was a bit tumbledown and it was always a bit of a struggle to play at your best in those surroundings.

Steaua Bucharest's Steaua Stadium wasn't exactly Celtic Park or the Westfalen either. It was pretty ramshackle as well and presumably because of drainage problems or whatever there was a terrible smell in the dressing-room. It wasn't the kind of ground you would want to play at every week.

I played in Riga for Scotland against Latvia and in some ways it wasn't dissimilar to Bucharest, which really says it all. And the last of the not-so-magnificent seven would have to be Hansa Rostock's Ostsee Stadium. They were an East German club from the 'other side' of the old Berlin Wall, of course, and it showed. Their facilities were pretty primitive. If the first group of grounds was seven of the best then the others were definitely seven of the worst in my experience.

Now to referees. I think it's fair to say in the first instance that I wouldn't do their job for any amount of money. It's bad enough being a player and playing the game and being booed and jeered by half the crowd at some games, but when everyone in the stadium has a go at you at some point it can't be much fun. Officials get it from all quarters. Players have a pop at them and supporters, of course, are never happy. They are on a hiding to nothing from the outset and there's no way you would get me out there doing their job.

As it happens, I believe that in the main referees are pretty good in Scotland. I know they take a lot of stick from so-called experts in newspapers and on radio and television but on the whole I have found them to be pretty fair. Clearly there are exceptions, as there are in any country, but I have to say I believe they give decisions as they see them. It's all done in a split second, remember, and there is no going back. There is also no instant television evidence showing the decision from a dozen different angles. It's always easy to criticise when you can look at an offside decision 20 times and then again in slow motion and then again by freezing the picture. But referees don't have any of those luxuries. Inevitably mistakes are made, but by and large I reckon they're genuine ones and over the course of the season they probably balance themselves out between players and teams.

In Scotland, I think guys like Jim McCluskey, Hugh Dallas – in spite of him ordering me off early in the 1998–99 season – and Kenny Clark are among the best. I've been pretty impressed with them on the occasions they've taken Celtic games, although I suppose they might not have noticed that at the time! Forgive me if I don't mention the names of the ones I think are the worst . . .

What I would like to see, though, and what I think would make the standard higher generally is professional, full-time referees. I just feel that with players being professional, the officials should be as well. They are currently not paid that much for the abuse they take and they all, out of necessity, have other jobs. I believe if they were paid properly and could train in more or less the way full-time players do they would be consistently better.

I also think it would be a good idea if we had an élite group of those top professional officials who did the Premier League games on some kind of rota system. They would get to know players better that way and maybe be able to understand and appreciate more what goes on.

What I can never envisage coming into being, however, is the suggestion of FIFA president Sepp Blatter, who reckons it would be a good idea for ex-professional players to become referees when they retire. The theory might be fine, but of all the players I have come across in my time I can't think of any who would fancy the idea. In fact, it's too ludicrous a suggestion to think about. Imagine me finishing playing and trying to be a referee. Even if I could do it, I certainly wouldn't want to. Mind you, I think it is Mr

Blatter who also fancies the idea of doing away with tackling in the game so maybe we shouldn't take his ideas too seriously.

The really worrying thing about all that is that he is the sport's main man. I don't profess to understand how some officials reach their exalted positions in the game, nor, indeed, how some directors reach the boardroom. There again, maybe they wonder how on earth I became a player.

Talking of which, I've trawled around the Premier League clubs looking for Scottish players whom I rate really highly and before I give an opinion – and, remember, that's what all of this is – let me say that I kept away from my own club.

I should also add that my recent experience is limited because I've only been back in the country for a wee while, and that I'm talking here about players whose style I personally like. There are lots of quality players but since this is my book I can make the choices!

And, in fact, it's actually a single choice rather than several choices. It may even surprise some people, but I happen to think Eoin Jess is an outstanding player. I remember him bursting on to the scene a few years ago – in tandem with Scott Booth – and I think he would probably accept that he hasn't done himself full justice since. Yet he has quality written all over him and there are definite signs at Aberdeen that he is beginning to fulfil all that potential. I just think that Eoin is a tremendous offensive player who can pass and score. He is very aware and has a good touch. It's not really for me – even with my opinions – to say where he should be played but I feel that his best position is just behind the front two, where his vision would be vital.

He has no real defensive qualities that I can think of particularly, but there again other players in the team can take care of that side of things and let him get on with the job of hurting the opposition at the other end of the park. He is good at that – just as long as he doesn't do it against Celtic!

So there it is, a comprehensive look at some of what's right and wrong in Scottish football . . . with one notable exception. This will not please some people but there is no doubt in my mind that Celtic and Rangers are far too big for Scottish football. The Old Firm has outgrown the domestic scene and it's time they moved on to pastures new. Some kind of European league is obviously the answer and although it's been talked about a lot over the years, and again very recently in England, I'm sorry to say I'm not sure it will happen in my football lifetime.

I can just imagine people from Dumfries to Dundee and all around the country cracking up at the very suggestion that Glasgow's big two are above it all and so on, but I have become more and more convinced that that is indeed the case. Certainly, I feel that the rest of the clubs in Scottish football need Celtic and Rangers more than Celtic and Rangers need them. The two clubs attract attendances far beyond even the wildest dreams of the others. One home crowd at either of the Old Firm grounds is more than many clubs get in a season, and that is surely ludicrous. Those massive 50,000-plus attendances are also, I might add, better than any club in England with the exception of Manchester United.

That alone would surely be enough for any neutral to understand the need for change. But look as well at the two grounds, Celtic Park and Ibrox, which are superb. They lend themselves to bigger and better things. I don't profess to know what would be the solution to the problems that would inevitably accompany any attempt by the Old Firm to leave this country, but one possibility might be to have one squad in a regular Euro league and another operating in Scotland. I can see something like that coming.

And from a player's point of view it would be fantastic. Any good professional wants to better himself and one way of doing that is to compete against better players at a higher level. That would do for me. Imagine playing Ajax in Amsterdam one week, then being at home to Borussia

Dortmund and then away again to Inter Milan. No one could say anything other than the fact it would be sensational.

The fans, too, would love it, I'm sure. It would be fresh and different and Celtic supporters would relish trips to the foreign cities. They seem to find their way in huge numbers to wherever we play, and it would be great for them.

I also happen to believe that both Celtic and Rangers would hold their own in such exalted company. I know that recent European results haven't been very clever and certainly haven't backed up that view, but playing at that level on a regular basis would lead to improvement and standards would therefore rise. That isn't always the case on the domestic front, where players and teams are so familiar with each other it can become predictable and even boring.

The Old Firm has to get out of Scotland, and whether or not it happens in my time I think it is inevitable. If – or when – they do, it might even be possible for one of them to again win something in Europe. Currently, I have to say I don't think either really has a serious chance because of our domestic demands.

My greatest success, of course, was unquestionably winning the European Cup with Borussia Dortmund but I have to be honest and say I'm not sure a Scottish club will ever be able to achieve that honour now, at least not in the foreseeable future. Celtic did it in 1967 and maybe the very fact that the feat will probably never be repeated in my opinion makes the efforts of Billy McNeill, John Clark, Ronnie Simpson, Bobby Murdoch, Jimmy Johnstone, Bertie Auld and company even greater. Rangers have already had a few stabs at it in recent times and so, for that matter, have Celtic, with much the same level of success – or lack of it.

The odds are stacked against a Scottish success nowadays simply because the big clubs in Europe seem to have more going for them. They can attract better players generally and appear to have endless supplies of cash to back their Euro bids. The Old Firm are wealthy by Scottish standards but put them in the bigger league and it is all put into perspective. They need that kind of higher-class competition regularly – and soon.

Anyway, all that aside, when I was talking to co-author Graham Clark about the players I have played with and against during my time at St Mirren, Motherwell, Borussia and Celtic, he stumbled on the idea of making me a manager for a moment and asked me to pick two teams from players I have played alongside and those I've been in opposition to at club level.

Now I know I'll never be a Wim Jansen or a Craig Brown! The task was close to impossible and I realise why these managerial guys have sleepless nights. At least my selections – or the players I have left out, anyway – won't get the chance to have tantrums or demand transfers, but I'll probably upset a few guys along the way anyway!

We started with a squad of players I have played alongside and it was unbelievably difficult from the word go to sort out 16 names from the dozens of fine team-mates I've had over the years. My side eventually lined up like this: Stefan Klos; Stefan Reuter, Jurgen Kohler, Matthias Sammer, Julio Cesar, Jorg Heinrich; Paulo Sousa, Andy Möller, Craig Burley; Karl-Heinz Riedle, Stephane Chapuisat. Substitutes: Campbell Money, Alan Stubbs, Michael Zorc, Vladimir But, Simon Donnelly.

Going from back to front we start with Klos, and it was easy for me to see why Rangers were so keen to sign the big man as a successor to Andy Goram. He has a tremendous presence about him and that gave him, and the players in front of him, great confidence. He had a superb season the year I was at Dortmund and, like Goram, saved the team a few points on his own.

At the back it's really no surprise I have gone for four Germans and then a Brazilian international to finish it all off. All the German lads are, well, typically German. They're strong and efficient and have a tremendous mentality when it comes to winning at football. You've seen their successes over the years and it's that mentality that has carried them through a lot of difficult times.

They have plenty of other attributes into the bargain. Reuter is very quick and his pace is a huge asset at the back. Kohler is quite simply the best defender I have ever seen while Sammer is the nearest Germany has had to Franz Beckenbauer and Heinrich's qualities have most recently been recognised by Fiorentina, who paid a fortune to land him. Now add Julio Cesar, who is a marvellous player. He is a mountain of a bloke but has a tremendous touch. He can win the ball and play it in one movement and I had to find room for him in the team. I just couldn't leave him out.

And that is what I call a defence. Perry Mason couldn't be any better. I couldn't see that lot losing many goals.

Yet if it was difficult to settle on players in defence, it was virtually impossible to select guys for the middle of the park. I was hit by an embarrassment of riches for the midfield department. In the end I went for what I believe is a good mix. Paulo simply had to get in because he is a wonderful talent. He was injured in my early days at Dortmund – which, ironically, was probably good news for me because his absence allowed me to get a game – but when he was fit, not too many could touch him for skill.

Maybe, having said that, Möller could! Andy, as I've mentioned elsewhere, could win games out of nothing. He is an exceptionally gifted player and it was wonderful experience to play beside him.

And then there's Craig. The fact that he was my room-mate at the World Cup in France is neither here nor there! Seriously, he is a very good player. He won the Scottish Football Writers' Player of the Year award in the 1997–98 season and although I don't always agree with the media I have to say they got it exactly right then. His goals for Celtic as we won the Premier League were always great and usually crucial. I would like to see him get a run in midfield for Scotland because it's been well documented that that's his favourite position.

Up front, Riedle and Chapuisat are dynamite. Both are perhaps a little underestimated at times but when you play alongside them and see the runs they make off the ball as well as the work they do on it, together with the goals they score, you know you're playing with special players. I don't think there's a defence in the world that would feel entirely comfortable facing that pair.

The bench was a nightmare as well. Campbell Money will probably be a surprise inclusion but he was a hugely underestimated player and when I was at St Mirren I cannot recall many better goalkeepers. He was included in a few Scotland squads but never won a cap, and that was a shame because he deserved that recognition.

Zorc and But are simply quality. The German has a huge plus factor in the number of goals he can score from the middle of the park, while the Russian is a formidable force in the same area. Both had strong claims to be in the starting line-up but I can only play 11. Anyway, as all the best coaches tell you, it's a squad game nowadays and they both have a role to play.

Similarly, so do big Al and Sid. Stubbs has done so well for Celtic since he came north and I am convinced he deserved a chance with England. For the moment at least, though, he'll have to make do with my team – and I hope he's honoured to be in it!

I'm totally convinced that Simon will be a hugely influential player for club and country in the coming years. He has been a bit unlucky to find himself on the bench for Celtic on and off over the last season or so but at least that means he will be used to it in my squad.

That would do me for a 16-man squad any time – or would it? When it came to selecting players I have played against, I found myself getting a bit excited about that pool as well!

Here is that squad: Andy Goram; Jackie McNamara,

Lothar Matthaus, Paolo Montero, Lilian Thuram, Christian Ziege; Zinedine Zidane, Milinko Pantic, Thomas Hassler; Alessandro del Piero, Alen Boksic. Substitutes: Angelo Peruzzi, Taribo West, Christian Vieri, Henrik Larsson, Gheorghe Hagi. See what I mean? There are a few more-than-useful players in that lot and at least the same number again left out.

Let's start with Goram and, as I've said, I can well understand how former Celtic manager Tommy Burns became a bit frustrated with Andy. He always seemed to reserve some of his best performances for Old Firm matches. He was an outstanding goalkeeper for Rangers and, for that matter, Scotland. He beat off a lot of competition for a place in this team but he deserves to be there.

Jackie is a marvellous young talent who will surely go all the way in the game. And before anyone says he should have been in my other team, let me remind you that I played against Jackie before either of us were at Celtic.

The rest of the back lot would take a bit of getting past, that's for sure. Height, strength, craft, guile, grit and unbelievable ability – they have the lot, and that will do for me.

Matthaus, I have to say, was a better midfield man than he is a defender, which says something about his ability. He was close to the complete midfield man before he stepped back to continue to do wonderfully well. He is such an experienced player.

Montero is not a guy you would want to tangle with. Not at any price. He's as hard as nails and, let's face it, has to have been able to do something right to have played for Juventus.

Thuram showed at the World Cup just how good he is and by weighing in with two goals in the semi-final against Croatia the Parma man instantly became one of the true stars of the show. But even before then he looked good when I played against him.

Ziege is very strong and when I was at Dortmund I always liked the look of him when we came across Bayern Munich. He was a terrific buy for them, costing something like just £12,000 back in 1990.

Midfield is an area of the park I like to think I know a little bit about, and my trio there is awesome. Zidane is exceptional, as he proved in the World Cup final when he scored with two headers – and that isn't anything like the strongest part of his game. All that does, of course, is emphasise what a talent he is generally

Pantic I have talked about elsewhere and he can consider himself fortunate to be in the team because he made a donkey out of me once! Hassler, like my other midfielders, wears that number ten jersey that always catches my eye and he is one of the ones who fills it best. The three of them can fight it out to see who wears ten in my team. I certainly wouldn't like to choose!

Del Piero is incredibly gifted and he is eminently capable of winning a match on his own, which is a useful attribute for any team. He would combine well with Boksic, who is strong and quick and has a great eye for goal.

As for the bench, all have a claim to be in from the start but you can't please all of the people all of the time. I'm not even going to try. They certainly gave me more than adequate cover in a variety of areas.

Peruzzi is an excellent keeper who has enjoyed a wonderful career and would be in the running for any team. West, a big Nigerian, is a quite brilliant defender who impressed everyone at France '98 and even before then, for that matter.

Hagi is a legend in Romania and quite rightly so. He is a marvellous player who has been a huge influence on every team he's been with. Henrik is very clever and versatile and he has been a huge hit at Celtic. He had a terrific season last year and was one of the main reasons we won the league and Coca-Cola Cup double. Vieri is a first-class finisher and an all-round class act. He showed just how good he is at

France '98 as well, and that tournament did a few reputations some good.

What a game it would be to put one team against the other. Imagine del Piero against Sammer or Riedle against Matthaus. Or how about the midfield battle between Zidane and Möller? The possibilities are endless. I'm a novice at this selection lark but I don't think there's a manager or a coach in the world who wouldn't take either of those sides at the drop of a hat.

It would be well-nigh impossible to put a value on these players in the current transfer market but you wouldn't get much change from £100 million for either team. Indeed, the only problem I can see in all this is that I can't get a game myself!

It's impossible to imagine the wages involved for all these players, and the question of money in the game has caused a fair old row at Celtic Park this season. I'll come to that later, but I do feel there is a significant background to the vexed question of cash in football generally.

Chairmen and directors will vouch for the fact that one of the biggest things in modern-day football is sponsorship and when you look around you actually wonder how clubs survived without it in the bad old days. Celtic are handed millions of pounds by Umbro, Rangers have McEwan's Lager, Hibs are tied in with Carlsberg, Arsenal have JVC, Manchester United go with Sharp and even Scotland have Scottish Gas. Clubs and countries take full advantage, as they are perfectly entitled to.

Sponsors range from big multi-national companies to local bakeries, but it is important to remember that none are in the business of being charitable. They don't just hand over their cash – be it large amounts or small – and watch it being banked by happy commercial managers up and down the country. Sponsorship is a two-way street. These companies want their money's worth and that's why more and more you will see some of the above names at every turn where your club is concerned. They will milk it for all it's worth and when television is involved the stakes are even higher. The exposure the companies get from even fleeting glimpses of a player's shirt are worth fortunes. It is big, big business.

Players, too, get their fair share and some walk about like advertising boards! One or two I can think of look more like grand prix drivers, who seem to have a company logo on every part of their gear, than footballers.

Personally, I am not a great believer in doing too much in the way of sponsorship. There have been a few offers made to me over the years – especially since I was at Borussia Dortmund – but it's just not my style to get too involved.

The one concession I have made to it is to sign a three-year deal with Diadora to wear their boots. When I played in Germany I wore Nike because they had a deal with Dortmund which covered the players as well. Everyone was in the same boat – or should that be boot! When I came back to Scotland I used adidas, Puma or anything else I liked the feel of. I was never too fussy about the brand name as long as they were comfortable and I felt they were right.

Then, out of the blue, I received a telephone call from the British rep for Diadora, asking me if I would be interested in trying their product. Nothing ventured, nothing gained, as they say, and I wore them first on the day back in February when Harald Brattbakk scored four goals against Kilmarnock. I can't remember them doing much for me that afternoon but Harald must have liked the sight of them!

In fact, Diadora gave me half a dozen pairs of different styles to try in training and in games and I found I was pretty happy with them the longer the season went on. It is vital for a player to feel really comfortable because if he has any kind of problem with something like his boots he can't possibly be right for a match. It's maybe more important than some people might imagine.

In due course I was pleased when Diadora offered me a deal. They flew me out to their factory near Venice at the end of the season and I must admit that was a bit of an eye-opener. It was an impressive place and if I had been in any doubt beforehand about the stature of the company I wasn't after I had set foot inside.

Equally as impressive as the set-up were the people. They are obviously vastly experienced and professional people and they leave no stone unturned to make sure that things are just right for the individual player, athlete or sportsman or woman.

They use some sort of pressure-pad to measure your feet, take photographs of them and generally leave nothing to chance. The net result is a football boot that feels like a comfortable shoe and I now have a stock of my own individual boots bearing the legend 'PL – 14'. I also know that I can get on the phone and get more specially made to the measurements they have at the factory in next to no time.

I'm not alone in having personalised boots, of course, because a lot of top players around the world have them and Diadora themselves deal with players like Roberto Baggio and Clarence Seedorf, plus a host of other big names.

I signed my three-year contract when I was out there and I have to say there was a fair bit of money involved for me to wear – and promote, when possible – their brand. But I would stress that I am genuinely not plugging Diadora for the money. It would be absolutely no use to me if they gave me a few quid and the boots were hopeless. That would ruin the whole point of the exercise. The boots are my priority. The money is secondary.

And I don't think I can exactly be accused of overdoing it in the sponsorship market because that is the only deal I have. I used to drive a Honda supplied via Celtic by a local garage but I returned that because I prefer to drive my own choice, and that is it.

Otherwise, both Celtic and Scotland use Umbro and they send gear to the players occasionally for when we are away before important matches or at the World Cup or whatever. It might not sound terribly worthwhile to some people for a company to give away clothes or boots but, believe me, they would soon stop it if they felt it wasn't in their own best interests. No one does anything for nothing in football.

And other sports latch on to sponsors big-time as well. I mentioned Formula One motor racing, which seems to be a sponsor's dream, but just about everyone is into it in some way. It can be subtle or it can be overpoweringly prominent, but however it's achieved it is generally noticed – and that, obviously, is what it's all about.

Sponsorship, of course, also helps to pay wages and transfer fees and I must say I find it incredible that we have now reached the stage where £15 million deals are almost commonplace in the game. I find it extraordinary that anyone can be worth that kind of money to play football and, it has to be said, it is also a bit obscene. Imagine what that amount of money would do for starving kids around the world, for instance.

Yet, as with so many things, it is a case of supply and demand in football. Clubs are desperate to get their hands on someone like Ronaldo or Alan Shearer and will pay whatever is required to get them. They know they are giving themselves more chances of success, and at the same time the commercial benefits are huge.

My only concern is where it will all end. At the moment football is buzzing. It's the in-thing, especially so in England, where the Premiership was recently named the biggest-spending league in the world. Money appears to be no object down south. The grounds are currently not big enough to take all the people who want to go to games, players are moving for astronomical sums of money and it is very much a golden era.

Unfortunately, in some ways it is also proving a problem. Big clubs are unquestionably getting bigger and the rest are trailing further and further behind. Manchester United, Arsenal, Liverpool, Chelsea and a couple of others are disappearing out of sight, which must be a real concern to others.

I just can't help feeling, too, that there will be a day of reckoning somewhere down the line and what will happen then? Football is no different from any other sport or pastime, really. When people get fed up with it, they will find something else to do. When the current gloss fades, as it will inevitably do at some point, there are bound to be casualties.

Clubs who have perhaps over-spent to increase the size of their stadium to accommodate the demands of the moment could find them half-full but with the same running costs. How do they get round that problem?

And it's not only the fans who may decide to turn their backs on the game at some point in the future. What if Jack Walker pulled the plug on Blackburn Rovers, or David Murray decided enough was enough at Rangers? Fergus McCann at Celtic has made no bones about the fact that he is only in Glasgow on a five-year plan and he is due to leave in the summer – with, presumably, a more than adequate return on his initial investment. As things stand, there will be other businessmen ready to replace these people, possibly even forming orderly queues to get involved, but if it all goes pear-shaped . . .

Don't get me wrong – it's great while it lasts and I have no wish to be a prophet of doom. Nor do I have the answers, before anyone asks. All I'm doing is sounding a note of caution, because if Wall Street can crash so can football.

Players, of course, are also milking the current boom for all it's worth and that doesn't make us any different from everyone else who is making money out of the game.

If I never thought I would hear of £15 million transfers, I certainly never believed for a second that players would be on £50,000 a week, as is alleged to be the case with some individuals in England. But what can you say, apart from good luck to them?

In the unlikely event of someone offering me £50,000 a week, I would find it hard to hesitate. Footballers have a relatively short working life and they have to take – or certainly look closely at – every opportunity that comes their way.

There was a well-documented row at Celtic Park early in the 1998–99 season about money and I have to say that one or two people were fairly economical with the truth at that time. I didn't believe then, and still don't, that the players were asking for anything they weren't entitled to. The club can't keep taking and not giving. It's like sponsorship – it's a two-way thing. All that may sound a bit greedy but I don't think the principles are any different from those in any other walk of life. And, yes, if the boom turns into bust then players will have to hold their hands up and accept their share of the blame. But as long as clubs are willing to pay big-money transfers and huge wages, players will accept it. The responsibilities lie all over the game.

It is important as well to remember that when I talk about those kind of figures, I'm talking about a relatively small number of clubs and players throughout the country. It's only the big names in the Premiership and, to a lesser extent, the Premier League in Scotland who are on big money. The guy in the Scottish Second Division or the Third Division down south isn't making a handsome living out of football. He may be barely earning a living at all, come to that. There are always two sides to every story and it's important not to forget that.

In the midst of all my concerns, though, I should say that right now it's great to be involved in the game from a playing and financial point of view. There is something very special about playing in front of 60,000 passionate fans more or less every week and getting well paid for that is the icing on the cake.

There are pressures, naturally, but they go with the territory. I can hardly complain about them because I will never lose sight of the fact that thousands upon thousands of people would love to do what I do. I know how lucky I am, and I appreciate it.